# Microsoft
# WINDOWS®
# 95
## *simplified!*

## TUTORIAL & APPLICATIONS ▪ ▪ ▪ ▪ ▪

Todd Knowlton
Computer Education Consultant

**JOIN US ON THE INTERNET**
WWW: http://www.thomson.com
EMAIL: findit@kiosk.thomson.com    A service of I(T)P®

**South-Western Educational Publishing**

*an International Thomson Publishing company* I(T)P®

Cincinnati • Albany, NY • Belmont, CA • Bonn • Boston • Detroit • Johannesburg • London • Madrid
Melbourne • Mexico City • New York • Paris • Singapore • Tokyo • Toronto • Washington

Managing Editor: Janie F. Schwark
Editor: Shannon O'Connor
Marketing Manager: Kent Christensen
Cover Design: Lou Ann Thesing
Electronic Prepress Production: A. W. Kingston Publishing

Copyright © 1997
by SOUTH-WESTERN EDUCATIONAL PUBLISHING
Cincinnati, Ohio

ISBN: 0-538-71628-2

4  5  6  PR  01  00  99  98

Printed in the United States of America

I(T)P®
International Thomson Publishing

South-Western Educational Publishing is a division of International Thomson Publishing Inc. The ITP logo is a registered trademark used herein under license by South-Western Educational Publishing.

# Preface

Microsoft Windows 95[1] is an easy-to-use operating system that provides many features of the most advanced operating systems, while retaining compatibility with existing software. Microsoft Windows 95 Simplified!: Tutorial and Applications is designed to make learning to use Windows 95 as easy as possible.

## TEXT OVERVIEW

This text is designed to familiarize you with the features and user interface of Windows 95 in 130 lessons grouped into 13 units. Each lesson builds on what was learned in previous lessons, reinforcing the concepts already learned.

- Unit 1 introduces Windows 95 and covers the basics of starting Windows, using the Start button, using menus, and shutting down windows.

- Unit 2 covers the manipulation of windows on the desktop. The unit includes opening and closing windows, maximizing and minimizing windows, and moving and resizing windows.

- Unit 3 introduces WordPad, the simple word processor included with Windows 95.

- Unit 4 presents the Windows Help system. Searching for help by contents and by index, and using find are covered. Obtaining help with button names and menu commands is also covered.

- Unit 5 provides further coverage of WordPad. The unit covers editing and formatting text, along with copying and moving text. The concepts learned while working with WordPad will be applicable when you use other Windows 95 word processors.

- Unit 6 introduces the My Computer icon. Viewing, selecting, copying, and moving items are covered. The unit ends with creating folders, opening and printing documents from an icon, and using Quick View.

- Unit 7 presents more desktop features including deleting files and folders, saving a document to the desktop, using the documents menu, and arranging the desktop. The unit also includes short-cuts and how to customize the taskbar.

- Unit 8 looks at the Explorer. In addition to browsing folders and copying and moving items, the unit covers formatting and copying disks and other file features.

- Unit 9 covers the Find command. Finding by name, location, date modified, file type, file size, and the text in a file are all covered.

- Unit 10 introduces Paint. The unit covers drawing lines and shapes, using colors, erasing, and adding text to paintings. Students will learn how to copy graphics created in Paint to other applications.

- Unit 11 presents some of the other Windows accessories and multimedia features. The Calculator, Calendar, Cardfile, Notepad, and Media Player are covered.

- Unit 12 covers the Control Panel. Accessing the Control Panel, using the Hardware Wizard, and adding and removing programs are covered. The Control Panel is used in Unit 12 to change display settings, add desktop patterns and wallpaper, turn on a screen saver, change mouse settings, and set the system date and time.

---

[1] Windows and Microsoft are registered trademarks of Microsoft Corporation.

# Preface

- Unit 13 presents system maintenance features and running DOS programs. Performing backups, using the disk defragmenter, and using ScanDisk are all covered in the unit.

- Appendix A presents networking concepts and the Microsoft Network online service.

- Appendix B describes the Windows 95 accessibility options for disabled computer users or those who need assistance when interacting with the computer.

The Instructor's Manual provides teaching suggestions and solutions to the book's activities.

## ACKNOWLEDGMENTS

Many people helped make this book a reality. In addition to the people at South-Western, I thank Tre' Church, Eric Hosch, and Bryan Stephens for their contributions to the manuscript, and Mark Durrett for his careful technical review of this text. I also thank Jonathan Sooter for his review of the book's early lessons from a student's perspective.
A special thank you goes to Jeff Bateman for creating the video clip used to demonstrate the media player.

*Todd Knowlton*

# Contents

# Contents

# Introduction

## Learning Objective

A clearly defined learning objective helps you understand about the new skill.

## Units

Unit numbers are clearly indicated on each lesson.

## Quick Reference Bar

Emphasizes easy-to-use tips and important information to note.

---

**UNIT 3**

LESSON

**29**

**Changing Settings in WordPad**

In this lesson, you will learn to change settings in WordPad.

▶ **SKILL PRACTICE**

TIP  The other sections of the Options dialog box allow you to set options for the various file formats supported by WordPad.

### To Show or Hide Screen Elements

1.  With the United Nations document open in WordPad, pull do the **View** menu. Notice that the first four items on the menu h check marks by them. These are the currently visible screen elements.

2.  Choose **Format Bar**. The check mark disappears and the for bar is hidden.

3.  Choose **Ruler** from the **View** menu. The check mark disappe and the ruler is hidden.

4.  Choose **Format Bar** from the **View** menu. The check mark reappears, and the format bar is shown again.

5.  Choose **Ruler** from the **View** menu. The check mark reappea and the ruler is shown again.

### To Change the Unit of Measurement

6.  Choose **Options** from the **View** menu. The Options dialog bo appears. The various sections of the dialog box are accessible clicking the tabs near the top of the dialog box.

7.  Click the **Options** tab. The Options section of the dialog box appears.

8.  Click the **Centimeters** measurement unit option button.

9.  Click **OK**. Notice the ruler now shows centimeters rather tha inches.

10. Choose **Options** from the **View** menu.

11. Click the **Options** tab.

12. Change the measurement unit back to inches and click **OK**.

62

**UNIT 3**  Introduction to Wor

## Skill Practice

A step-by-step, hands-on exercise walks you through a specific skill so that you can learn the task by doing it.

## Glossary Terms

Introduces and reinforces vocabulary
relevant to the lesson.

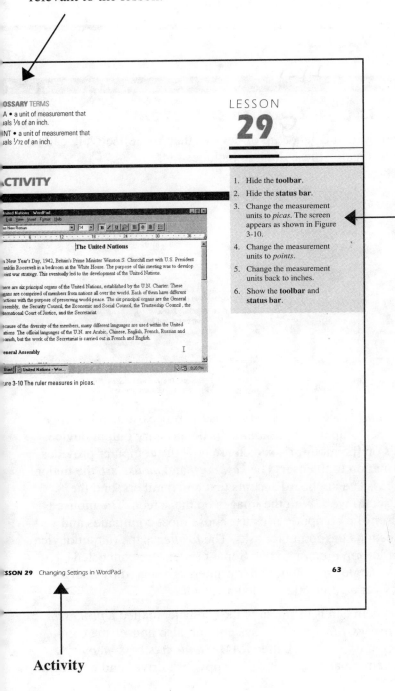

## Activity Directions

Clear, concise directions
to ensure success in applying
learned skills.

## Activity

An exercise to help you
further develop the new skill
and previously learned skills.

## End of Unit Exercises

Most units end with:

A Reinforcement Exercise that
incorporates a review of previously
learned skills.
A Challenge Exercise that utilizes
decision-making.

1

# LESSON 1

**Your Computer's Hardware**

In this lesson, you will learn about the components that make up a computer.

## ►CONCEPT LESSON

## The Parts of a Computer System

A computer system is made up of devices that are collectively called *hardware*. Typically, these devices include:

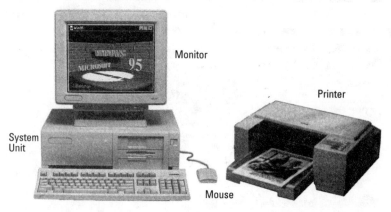

Figure 1-1 Parts of a Computer System

**NOTE** The term *central processing unit* (or CPU) is sometimes used to describe the entire system unit, not just the processor in the system unit.

The *system unit* is the case that contains the processing and storage devices of the computer. The *monitor* is the primary output device. The images on the monitor's screen are how the computer provides most information to the user. The *keyboard* and *mouse* are the major input devices. The keyboard accepts text and numbers, and the mouse is used to work with the images on the screen. The mouse is what the user of a computer uses to choose most commands and answer questions the computer asks. The *printer* is the output device used to put information on paper. Some printers are connected directly to a single computer. Other printers are shared by many computers over a connection called a *network*.

Inside the system unit is the brain of the computer (called a *processor* or *central processing unit*). The system unit also houses the computer's temporary storage, called *RAM* (*random access memory*), and the more permanent storage of floppy disk drives and hard disk drives.

Many computer systems also include a *fax modem* for going online and communicating by fax, a *CD-ROM drive* for accessing information on compact disc, and speakers for quality sound output.

## GLOSSARY TERMS

HARDWARE • the devices that make up a computer system.

SYSTEM UNIT • the case that holds the processing and storage devices of the computer

MONITOR • the computer's video display

KEYBOARD • the device used to input text and numbers into the computer

MOUSE • a hand-held input device that allows you to point to and select items on the screen.

# ►ACTIVITY

1. What devices are found in the system unit?

2. What is the computer's primary output device?

3. What device puts information on paper?

4. RAM is an acronym for:

5. List two input devices.

   a. _____

   b. _____

## MORE GLOSSARY TERMS

PRINTER • an output device that puts text and images on paper

NETWORK • two or more computers connected by a communications link

CENTRAL PROCESSING UNIT (CPU) • the device that is the brain of the computer

RANDOM ACCESS MEMORY (RAM) • a computer's temporary storage

FAX MODEM • a device that allows computers to communicate and send and receive faxes via telephone lines

CD-ROM DRIVE • a device that allows computers to access data stored on compact disc

UNIT 1

LESSON

2

Software and Operating
Systems

In this lesson, you will learn about
the instructions that make a
computer work.

## ►CONCEPT LESSON

## Software

As you learned in the previous lesson, a computer is a collection of devices that work together to process and store information and interact with the user. Computers, however, must be told what to do. The instructions a computer follows are known as *software*.

A word processor, spreadsheet program, or game is a type of software called *application software*. Application software performs the tasks you want the computer to do. For example, application software is what you use to produce a document or balance your checkbook. It takes more than application software, however, to make a computer run. Application software relies on another type of software, called *system software,* to control the hardware.

System software coordinates the interaction of the hardware devices, controls the input and output, and loads application software into memory so that you can run the programs you want to run. The system software required to run your computer is most often packaged together and called an *operating system.*

## Operating Systems

In computing today, knowing the operating system a computer is using is more important than knowing the manufacturer of the computer itself. Application software is generally categorized by the operating system on which it runs. For example, a program may be categorized as an MS-DOS program, a Windows 95 program, an OS/2 program, or a MacOS program. All of these are operating systems that run on personal computers.

The operating system serves as a foundation for the application software, and application software inherits characteristics from the operating system. For example, if an operating system allows you to name files with long descriptive names, then the application software may also allow long filenames.

**NOTE** Some computers are capable of running more than one type of operating system. Many computers, however, support only one type of operating system.

GLOSSARY TERMS

SOFTWARE • the instructions a computer follows

APPLICATION SOFTWARE • the programs that perform useful tasks for the user

SYSTEM SOFTWARE • the software needed to control the hardware and load application software

OPERATING SYSTEM • the system software required to run an entire computer system

LESSON

2

## ►ACTIVITY

1. Give two examples of types of application software.

   a. _____

   b. _____

2. Why is system software necessary?



3. List four operating systems.

   a. _____

   b. _____

   c. _____

   d. _____

**UNIT 1**

LESSON

**3**

**Introducing Windows 95**

In this lesson, you will learn about the Windows 95 operating system.

►**CONCEPT LESSON**

## Graphical User Interface

**NOTE** The acronym for Graphical User Interface (GUI) is pronounced "gooey."

Windows 95 is an operating system that communicates with the user through a *graphical user interface (GUI)* that makes the computer easy to use. A GUI displays buttons, icons, menus, and other controls on the screen. Using the mouse, the user can operate the computer by interacting with the images on the screen. Like other operating systems, Windows 95 includes the system software your computer needs to run. In addition, Windows 95 includes convenient accessories and programs that help you maintain your computer system and make the computer more useful.

Windows 95 makes it easy to start programs. You can even run more than one program at a time. You can switch between programs and transfer information between programs. Windows 95 also includes features that allow you to network computers together, use a fax modem to communicate with other computers over telephone lines, access the Internet, and send and receive faxes.

Organizing files is made easier with a GUI operating system. Tiny pictures, called *icons*, are used to represent the files stored on the computer's disks. A system of drives and folders is used to organize the files. Copying and deleting files can be accomplished without using the keyboard to enter a command.

The graphical abilities of Windows 95 make it a good operating system for *multimedia applications*. You can play sound files and video clips, record sounds, and play compact discs. Windows 95 also includes programs to help with common tasks, such as a calculator, a calendar, a notepad, a word processor, a painting program, and a card file.

# ►ACTIVITY

1. What kind of user interface does Windows 95 provide?

2. What device is used to interact with the images on a graphical user interface?

3. What is an icon?

4. List two of Windows 95's multimedia features.

   a. _____

   b. _____

5. List three of the programs included with Windows 95 to perform common tasks.

   a. _____

   b. _____

   c. _____

## ►SKILL PRACTICE

### Starting Windows

1. After the computer performs its startup tests, Windows 95 will begin to load. After Windows loads, you may be presented with a Welcome message, called a *dialog box*, as shown in Figure 1-2.

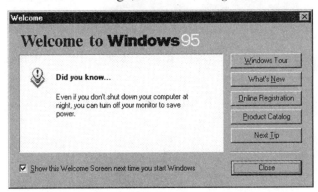

Figure 1-2 The Welcome Dialog Box

TIP
You can prevent the Welcome dialog box from appearing on startup by clearing the check box near the bottom left corner of the dialog box.

2. If you received the Welcome dialog box, press the Enter key to close the dialog box. The Windows *desktop* appears. Your screen should appear similar to Figure 1-3.

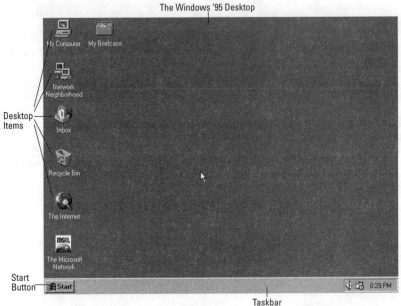

Figure 1-3 The Windows Desktop

*(continued on next page)*

GLOSSARY TERMS

DIALOG BOX • a window that gives information or requests input from the user

DESKTOP • the background against which the windows and icons appear

## ►ACTIVITY

Match the terms in the list below to the appropriate definition.

a. icons

b. system software

c. network

d. system unit

e. graphical user interface

f. operating system

g. dialog box

h. mouse

__h__ 1. A hand-held input device that allows you to point to and select items on the screen.

__g__ 2. A window that gives information or requests input from the user.

__e__ 3. A way of interacting with a computer by way of graphic images and controls.

__D__ 4. The case that holds the processing and storage devices of a computer.

__b__ 5. The software needed to control the hardware and load application software.

__f__ 6. The system software required to run an entire computer system.

__c__ 7. Two or more computers connected by a communication line.

__A__ 8. Tiny pictures used to represent files and to identify controls.

*Skill Practice* (continued)

The important parts of the Windows desktop are the desktop items, the taskbar, and the Start button. You will learn about these parts of the desktop in other lessons in this unit.

## ►SKILL PRACTICE

The basic mouse operations are point, click, right-click, double-click, and drag.

### Point

1. Position the mouse on the desk or mouse pad.

2. Move the mouse on the desk or mouse pad and watch the corresponding movement of the pointer on the screen.

3. Position the pointer over the time in the lower right corner of the screen. Do not press or click either mouse button. After a short delay, the day and date appear. This operation is called *pointing*.

### Click

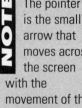

4. Point to the **My Computer** icon.

5. Quickly press and release the left mouse button one time. The My Computer icon changes color to indicate that it had been selected. This operation is called *clicking*.

6. Point to the **Recycle Bin** icon and click. The Recycle Bin is now selected.

### Double-Click

7. Point to the **My Computer** icon.

8. Quickly press and release the left mouse button twice. The My Computer icon will open and display a window of additional icons. This operation is called *double-clicking*.

9. Click the **X** (called the Close button) in the upper right corner of the My Computer window. The window closes.

### Drag

10. Point to the **My Computer** icon.

11. Press and hold down the left mouse button while the pointer is over the My Computer icon.

12. With the button held down, move the mouse to the right slightly. An image of the My Computer icon follows your pointer.

13. Move the pointer until it is approximately in the middle of the screen and release the mouse button. The icon moves to the new position. This operation is called *dragging*.

> **NOTE** The pointer is the small arrow that moves across the screen with the movement of the mouse. The appearance of the pointer changes depending on the area or type of object it is pointing at.

> **NOTE** *Clicking* refers to pressing and releasing the left mouse button. Some Windows operations will require you to click the right mouse button. This will be referred to as *right-clicking.*

LESSON

# 5

## ►ACTIVITY

Click Here to Close

Figure 1-4 The Recycle Bin Window

1. Point to the **Start** button in the lower left corner of the screen. The words *Click here to begin* appear. Do not click the mouse.

2. Point to the **Recycle Bin** icon.

3. Click the **Recycle Bin** icon to select it.

4. Point to the **My Computer** icon in the middle of the screen.

5. Click the **My Computer** icon to select it.

6. Click in a blank area next to the My Computer icon to deselect it.

7. Double-click the **Recycle Bin** to open the Recycle Bin window.

8. Click the **X** (the Close button) in the upper right corner of the Recycle Bin window to close the window, as shown in Figure 1-4.

9. Drag the **My Computer** icon back to its original position at the upper left corner of the desktop.

# LESSON 6

**Using the Keyboard**

In this lesson, you will learn to use the keyboard with Windows.

## ►SKILL PRACTICE

### Locating Important Keys

1. Using Figure 1-5 as a guide, identify the functions keys, Ctrl key, Alt key, Esc key, Shift key, and Enter key on your keyboard.

2. Identify the *cursor* control keys on your keyboard (see Figure 1-5).

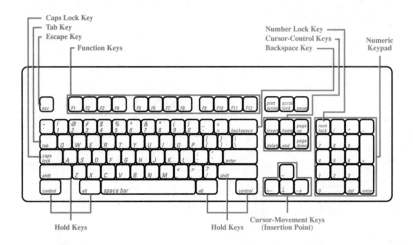

Figure 1-5 The Keyboard

### Using Keys Together

3. Hold down the **Alt** key.

4. With the **Alt** key held down, press and release the **S** key. The Start menu opens.

5. Press **Esc** to close the Start menu.

## ►ACTIVITY

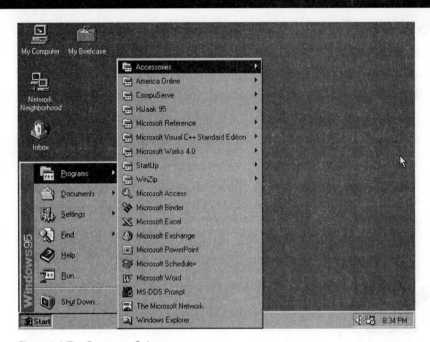

Figure 1-6 The Programs Submenu

1. Press **Alt+S** to open the
   Start menu.
2. Press the **down arrow** to
   highlight the first item in
   the menu.
3. Press the **right arrow** to
   access a submenu, as
   shown in Figure 1-6.
4. Press **Esc** to close the
   submenu.
5. Press **Esc** again to close the
   Start menu.

# LESSON

# 7

**The Start Button**

In this lesson, you will learn how to use the Start button to start programs.

## ►SKILL PRACTICE

**TIP**

If you allow the pointer to rest on an item that displays an arrow to the right of its description, or click on such an item, a submenu appears to provide more options. Multiple-level menus are often called cascading menus.

**NOTE**

Windows 95 allows more than one program to run at the same time.

## To Start Programs

1. With the mouse, point to the **Start** button at the lower left corner of the screen.

2. Click the left mouse button. The Start menu appears.

3. Move the pointer up and down within the menu. Notice how the item under the arrow is highlighted.

4. Point to the **Programs** item and allow the pointer to rest on it until the submenu appears.

5. Point to the **Accessories** item and wait for the Accessories menu to appear.

6. Click the **Notepad** accessory. The Notepad program loads and runs.

7. While leaving the Notepad open on your desktop, click the **Start** menu.

8. Click the **Programs** item.

9. Click the **Accessories** item.

10. Choose **Paint** from the **Accessories** menu. The Paint program loads and runs. The Notepad is moved to the background.

# ►ACTIVITY

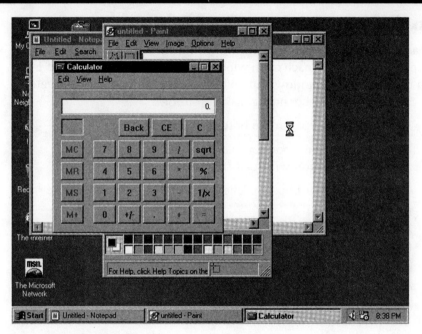

1. Open the **Start** menu.

2. Click the **Programs** item.

3. Click the **Accessories** item.

4. Start the **Calculator**. The other programs are moved to the background, as shown in Figure 1-7.

5. Leave the programs open and go on to Lesson 8.

Figure 1-7 The Calculator

UNIT 1

LESSON

8

Switching Between
Programs Using the
Taskbar

In this lesson, you will learn to use
the taskbar to switch between
programs.

# ►SKILL PRACTICE

## To Switch Between Programs

In addition to being the location of the Start button, the *taskbar* displays buttons for each open window or application (see Figure 1-8). An application or window can be brought to the front and activated by clicking the corresponding taskbar button.

1. Analyze the taskbar at the bottom of the screen.

2. Position the mouse pointer over the **Notepad** button on the taskbar. The button will read *Untitled - Notepad*.

3. Click the **Notepad** button. The Notepad becomes the active program.

4. Click the **Paint** button on the taskbar. The Paint program becomes active.

Figure 1-8 The Taskbar         Taskbar

GLOSSARY TERMS

TASKBAR • the bar that displays the
Start button, as well as buttons for each
open program and window.

LESSON

# 8

## ►ACTIVITY

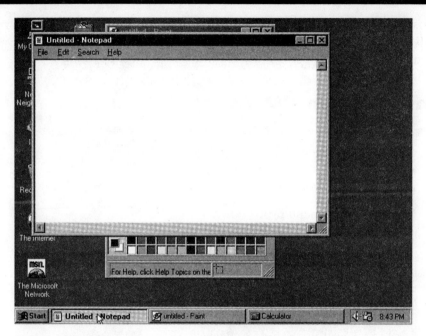

Figure 1-9 The taskbar allows you to switch quickly among programs.

1. Use the taskbar to switch to the **Calculator**.

2. Switch to the **Paint** program.

3. Switch to the **Notepad**. Your screen should appear similar to Figure 1-9. The sizes of your windows may vary from those in the figure.

4. Leave the **Calculator**, **Paint**, and **Notepad** open for the next lesson.

UNIT 1

LESSON

9

Using Menus

In this lesson, you will learn how to pull down a menu and choose a command.

## ►SKILL PRACTICE

Most commands in Windows programs are organized in menus that pull down from a program's menu bar. The *menu bar* is the row of menu names that appears below the title bar of most applications and windows.

### To Pull Down a Menu

The Notepad should be the active program on your screen.

1.  Click **File** on the menu bar (see Figure 1-10).
    Or
    Press **Alt+F**.

    Notepad's File menu drops down.

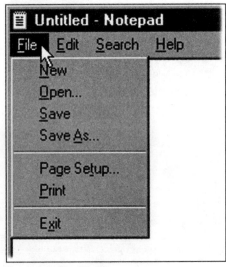

Figure 1-10 The File Menu

### To Close a Menu Without Choosing a Command

2.  Click somewhere outside the menu on the Notepad's work area.
    Or
    Press **Esc** (located at the top left corner of your keyboard). The File menu will close.

*(continued on next page)*

## ►ACTIVITY

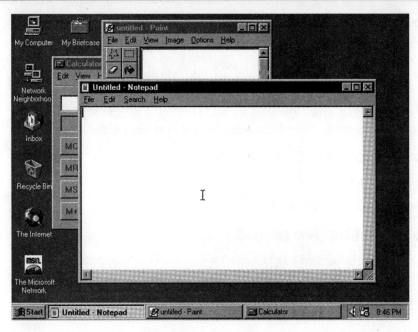

Figure 1-11 The New command cleared the Notepad.

1. Choose the **New** command
   from the **File** menu. A
   message appears asking if
   you want to save the
   changes to the current text.

2. Click the **No** button. The
   Notepad is cleared, as
   shown in Figure 1-11.

3. Leave the currently open
   applications open for the
   next lesson.

---

*Skill Practice (continued)*

## To Choose a Command

3. Pull down the **Edit** menu.

4. Move the pointer over the commands in the menu. Notice how
   each command is highlighted as the pointer passes over it.

5. Click the **Time/Date** command. The time and date appear in the
   Notepad.

LESSON

# 10

**Exiting a Program**

In this lesson, you will learn to exit programs.

## ►SKILL PRACTICE

### To Exit the Paint Program

1. Click the **Paint** button on the taskbar. The Paint program becomes active.

2. Click the **File** menu.

3. Choose **Exit** from the **File** menu. The Paint program is closed. Notice that the Paint button no longer appears on the taskbar.

### To Close the Calculator

4. Click the **Calculator** button on the taskbar.

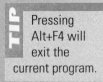

5. Click the Calculator's Close button.

### To Exit the Notepad

6. Click anywhere in the Notepad window. The Notepad becomes active.

7. Choose **Exit** from the **File** menu.

# ►ACTIVITY

1. Start the **Notepad**.

2. Choose **Time/Date** from the **Edit** menu.

3. Start the **Calculator**. Your screen should look similar to Figure 1-12.

4. Use the taskbar to switch to the **Notepad**.

5. Exit the **Notepad**. Do not save changes.

6. Close the **Calculator**.

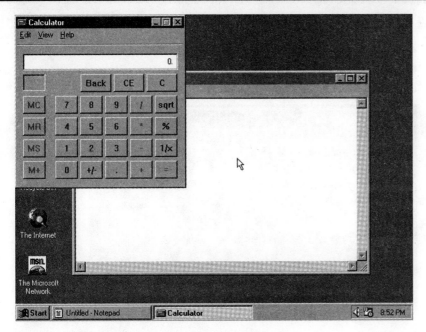

Figure 1-12 The Calculator appears on top of the Notepad.

LESSON

## 11

**Shutting Down Windows**

In this lesson, you will learn to shut down Windows 95.

# ►SKILL PRACTICE

**NOTE** Computers that are not on a network will not include the final shut down option shown in Figure 1-13.

**NOTE** The Shut Down dialog box gives you the option to shut down the computer, restart the computer, restart the computer in MS-DOS, or close all programs and log on as a different user (available on networks only). To choose one of the other options, click on the round button to the left of the desired option to select it.

## To Shut Down Windows

1. Access the **Start** menu.

2. Choose **Shut Down** from the **Start** menu. The Shut Down dialog box appears, as shown in Figure 1-13.

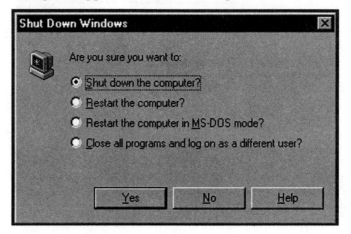

Figure 1-13 The Shut Down Dialog Box

3. Click **Yes** to shut down Windows 95.

4. When the message *It's now safe to turn off your computer* appears, turn off the computer.

# ►ACTIVITY

1. Turn on the computer.

2. After Windows 95 starts, start the **Notepad**.

3. Start the **Calculator**. Your screen should appear similar to Figure 1-14.

4. Exit the **Notepad**.

5. Close the **Calculator**.

6. Shut down Windows 95.

7. Turn off the computer.

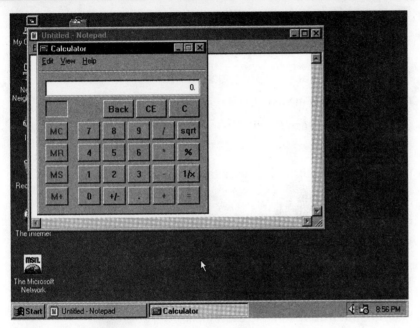

Figure 1-14 The Notepad and Calculator are running.

# Reinforcement Exercise

1. Turn on the computer. Wait for Windows 95 to start.

2. If necessary, close the Welcome dialog box.

3. When the desktop appears, click the **Recycle Bin** to select it.

4. Drag the **My Computer** icon to the right edge of the screen.

5. Drag the **Recycle Bin** to the space the My Computer icon formerly occupied.

6. Double-click the **Recycle Bin** to open it.

7. Pull down the **File** menu in the Recycle Bin window.

8. Choose the **Close** command from the Recycle Bin window's File menu.

9. Drag the **Recycle Bin** back to its original position.

10. Drag the **My Computer** icon back to its original position.

11. Start the **Calculator**.

12. Start the **Notepad**.

13. Switch to the **Calculator** using the taskbar.

14. Close the **Calculator**.

15. Exit the **Notepad**.

16. Choose **Shut Down** from the **Start** menu.

17. Choose the **Restart the computer** option.

18. Click **Yes**. The computer restarts and Windows 95 restarts.

# Challenge Exercise

G 1. Hardware

e 2. Application Software

d 3. System Software

h 4. Operating System

A 5. Central Processing Unit

I 6. Random Access Memory

J 7. Software

L 8. Graphical User Interface

O 9. Icons

B 10. Desktop

M 11. Dialog Box

K 12. Mouse

F 13. Cursor

C 14. Taskbar

n 15. Menu Bar

a. The brain of the computer.

b. The background against which the windows and icons appear.

c. The bar that displays the Start button, as well as buttons for each open program and window.

d. The software needed to control the hardware and to load application software.

e. The programs that perform useful tasks for the user.

f. The blinking vertical line that indicates the position at which the next character keyed will appear.

g. The devices that make up a computer system.

h. The system software required to run an entire computer system.

i. A computer's temporary storage.

j. The instructions a computer follows.

k. A hand-held input device that allows you to point to and select items on the screen.

l. A way of interacting with a computer by way of graphic images and controls.

m. A window that gives information or requests input from the user.

n. The bar below the title bar from which menus pull down.

o. Tiny pictures used to represent files and to identify controls.

Match the terms in the list to the appropriate definitions.

# LESSON 12

**The Elements of a Window**

In this lesson, you will learn the parts of windows.

## ►SKILL PRACTICE

### Parts of Windows

1. Double-click the **My Computer** icon.
2. Compare the window on your screen with Figure 2-1. The contents of the window will vary, depending on the configuration of your computer system.

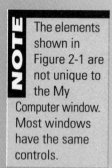

The elements shown in Figure 2-1 are not unique to the My Computer window. Most windows have the same controls.

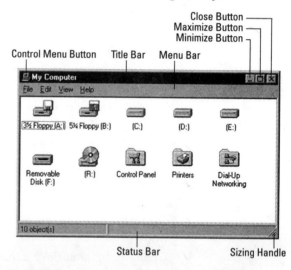

Figure 2-1 The Elements of a Window

Title bar - gives the name of the window or application
Menu bar - provides the menus for the commands available for working with an application or the contents of a window
Status bar - provides additional information about a command or highlighted object
Minimize button - removes a window from the desktop. The window is not closed and is still available from the taskbar.
Maximize button - enlarges a window to its maximum size
Close button - closes the window
Control menu button - accesses the control menu, which provides other window commands
Sizing handle - drag to resize the window manually

3. Leave the My Computer window open for the next lesson.

---

► ACTIVITY

---

1. What button enlarges a window to its maximum size?

2. What window element gives you the name of the window?

3. What button closes a window?

4. What window element allows you to resize a window manually?

5. What button removes a window from the desktop without closing it?

## LESSON
# 13

**Opening and Closing Windows**

In this lesson, you will learn how to open and close windows.

## ►SKILL PRACTICE

### To Open a Window

You can open a window by double-clicking its icon.

1. Double-click the **Recycle Bin**. The Recycle Bin window opens.

### To Close a Window

Close a window by clicking the window's Close button.

2. Click the Recycle Bin's **Close button**, as shown in Figure 2-2.

3. Click the My Computer window's **Close button**.

**TIP** You can also open a window by selecting the icon, clicking the right mouse button, and choosing Open from the resulting menu.

**TIP** You can also close a window by clicking the window's Control Menu button and choosing Close from the resulting menu.

Figure 2-2 The Close Button

---

## ►ACTIVITY

Figure 2-3 The Control Panel Window

1. Open the **My Computer** window.

2. Double-click the **Control Panel** folder icon in the My Computer window. The Control Panel window appears, as shown in Figure 2-3.

3. Close the **Control Panel** window.

4. Close the **My Computer** window.

# LESSON 14

**Maximize a Window**

In this lesson, you will learn how to maximize a window.

## ►SKILL PRACTICE

### To Maximize a Window

1. Open the **My Computer** window.

2. Click the *Maximize button*. The window fills the screen, as shown in Figure 2-4.

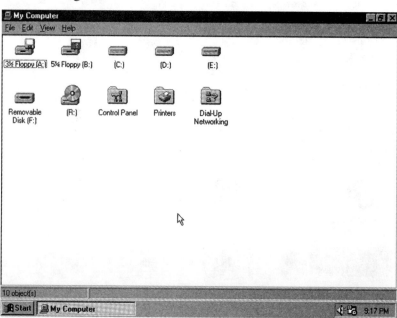

Figure 2-4 A Maximized Window

**NOTE** A maximized window fills the screen, leaving only the taskbar showing.

**GLOSSARY** TERMS

MAXIMIZE BUTTON • expands a
window to fill the screen.

►**ACTIVITY**

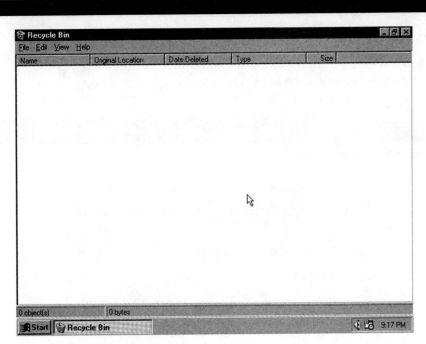

Figure 2-5 Maximized Recycle Bin

1. Close the **My Computer** window.

2. Open the **Recycle Bin** window.

3. Maximize the **Recycle Bin** window. Your screen should appear similar to Figure 2-5.

## ►SKILL PRACTICE

### To Restore a Window

When a window is maximized, the Maximize button becomes a *Restore button*, as shown in Figure 2-6.

Restore Button

Figure 2-6 The Restore Button

1. Click the **Restore** button on the Recycle Bin window.

2. Open the **My Computer** window. The window appears maximized.

3. Restore the **My Computer** window.

4. Close both windows.

> **NOTE**
> Restoring a maximized window returns it to the size it appeared before being maximized.

## ►ACTIVITY

Figure 2-7 The My Computer window has been restored.

1.  Open the **My Computer**
    window.

2.  Maximize the **My
    Computer** window.

3.  Restore the **My Computer**
    window. Your screen
    should look similar to
    Figure 2-7.

4.  Close the **My Computer**
    window.

**UNIT 2**

# LESSON
# 16

**Minimize a Window**

In this lesson, you will learn how to minimize and redisplay a window.

## ►SKILL PRACTICE

### To Minimize a Window

To temporarily remove a window from the desktop, you can minimize it.

1. Open the **My Computer** window.

2. Click the **Minimize** button, as shown in Figure 2-8. The window disappears. The window's name, however, still appears in the taskbar.

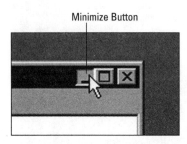

Minimize Button

Figure 2-8 The Minimize Button

### To Redisplay a Minimized Window

To redisplay a minimized window, click the window's button in the taskbar.

3. Click the **My Computer** button on the taskbar. The window reappears.

4. Close the **My Computer** window.

> **TIP**
>
> You can minimize all open windows by positioning the pointer over an empty area of the taskbar, clicking the right mouse button, and choosing Minimize All Windows from the resulting menu.

## ►ACTIVITY

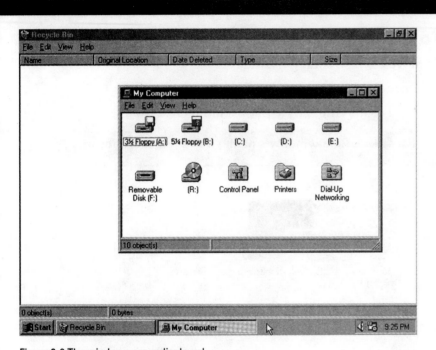

Figure 2-9 The windows are redisplayed.

1. Open the **Recycle Bin** window.

2. Maximize the **Recycle Bin** window.

3. Minimize the **Recycle Bin** window.

4. Open the **My Computer** window.

5. Minimize the **My Computer** window.

6. Redisplay the **Recycle Bin** window.

7. Redisplay the **My Computer** window (see Figure 2-9).

8. Restore the **Recycle Bin** window.

9. Close both windows.

# LESSON 17

**Move a Window**

In this lesson, you will learn how to move windows.

## ►SKILL PRACTICE

### To Move a Window

To move a window, drag its title bar.

1. Open the **My Computer** window.

2. Point to the **title bar**, as shown in Figure 2-10.

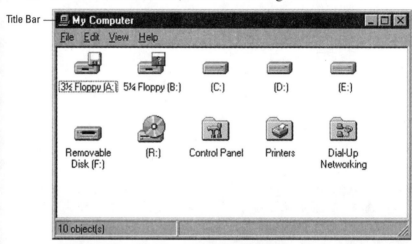

Title Bar

Figure 2-10 Move a window by dragging its title bar.

3. With the pointer on the **title bar**, press and hold the left mouse button.

4. With the mouse button held down, move the pointer to the right about 1 inch. You should see the window repositioned on your screen.

5. Release the mouse button.

6. Close the **My Computer** window.

> **TIP**
> When moving a window, do not drag from the top border of the title bar. If you do, you may accidentally resize the window rather than move it. You will learn how to resize windows in the next lesson.

►**ACTIVITY**

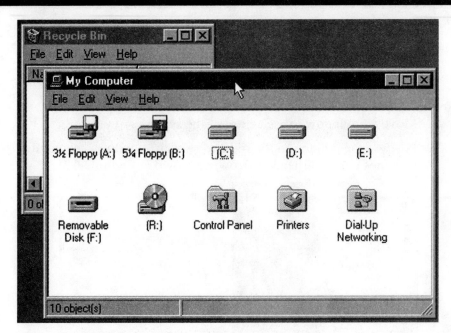

Figure 2-11 Windows may overlap each other.

1. Open the **Recycle Bin** window.

2. Maximize the **Recycle Bin** window.

3. Restore the **Recycle Bin** window.

4. Open the **My Computer** window.

5. If necessary, move the **My Computer** window over the **Recycle Bin** window (see Figure 2-11).

6. Move the **My Computer** window back to its original position.

7. Close both windows.

LESSON

# 18

**Resize a Window**

In this lesson, you will learn how to resize windows.

## ►SKILL PRACTICE

To resize a window, drag one of the window's edges or drag the sizing handle in the bottom right corner of the window.

### To Make a Window Wider

1.  Open the **Recycle Bin** window.

2.  Move the window to the center of the screen.

3.  Position the pointer on the right edge of the window. The pointer becomes a double-headed arrow, as shown in Figure 2-12.

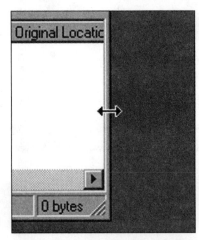

Figure 2-12 Positioning the pointer on an edge allows you to resize the window.

4.  Drag the right edge of the window until it is about 1 inch from the right edge of the screen.

5.  Drag the right edge of the window back approximately to its original position.

### To Make a Window Taller

6.  Position the pointer on the top or bottom edge of the window.

7.  Drag the edge up or down slightly to make the window taller.

*(continued on next page)*

**TIP**
You can change the width or height of a window from any edge of a window.

►**ACTIVITY**

1. Open the **My Computer** window.

2. Move and size the windows to make your screen closely match Figure 2-13.

3. Close both windows.

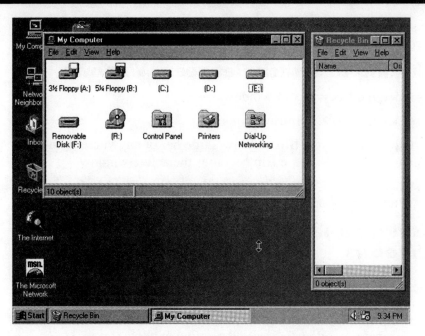

Figure 2-13 Moving and resizing windows allow you to place windows on the screen in a convenient arrangement.

*Skill Practice* (*continued*)

## To Change Height and Width at the Same Time

8. Position the pointer on the sizing handle in the bottom right corner of the window.

9. Drag the sizing handle down and to the right. The window becomes larger.

10. Drag the sizing handle up and to the left until the window is approximately its original size.

**TIP**
Any corner of the window can be used to resize the window. The bottom right corner, however, is the easiest to use because the pointer can be positioned correctly more easily.

**Switching Between Windows**

In this lesson, you will learn how to switch between windows.

## ►SKILL PRACTICE

To switch between windows, click on the window you want to become active or click the window's button on the taskbar.

### Clicking to Switch Between Windows

1. Open the **Recycle Bin** window.

2. Open the **My Computer** window.

3. Click the **Recycle Bin** window's title bar or anywhere in the window. The Recycle Bin becomes the active window.

4. Click the **My Computer** window's title bar. The My Computer window becomes the active window.

### Using the Taskbar to Switch Between Windows

5. Click the **Recycle Bin** button on the taskbar. The Recycle Bin becomes the active window.

6. Click the **My Computer** button on the taskbar. The My Computer window becomes the active window.

7. Close both windows.

# ►ACTIVITY

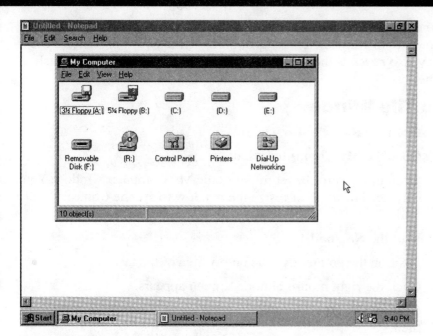

Figure 2-14 The Notepad is moved to the background.

1.  Open the **My Computer** window.

2.  Start the **Notepad**.

3.  Maximize the **Notepad**.

4.  Click the **My Computer** button on the taskbar. The My Computer window appears over the Notepad, as shown in Figure 2-14.

5.  Click in the **Notepad** window. The Notepad becomes active.

6.  Exit the **Notepad**.

7.  Close the **My Computer** window.

# LESSON
# 20

**Arranging Windows**

In this lesson, you will learn how to tile and cascade windows.

## ►SKILL PRACTICE

**NOTE** The Tile Horizontally command makes the windows tend to be wide. The Tile Vertically makes the windows tend to be tall.

When several windows are open at the same time, you can *tile* the windows to allow the contents of all the windows to be visible. You may also *cascade* the windows to stack them neatly on top of each other.

### To Tile Windows

1. Open the **Recycle Bin** window.

2. Open the **My Computer** window.

3. Open the Control Panel folder in the My Computer window. You may need to *scroll* or resize the window to see the Control Panel folder.

4. Start the **Notepad**.

5. Position the pointer over an empty area of the taskbar.

6. Click the right mouse button. A menu appears.

7. Choose **Tile Horizontally** from the menu. The windows are tiled.

**NOTE** Tiling and cascading resizes the windows involved. To return the windows to their original sizes, you must resize them manually.

### To Cascade Windows

8. Click the right mouse button on an empty area of the taskbar.

9. Choose **Cascade** from the menu. The windows are cascaded.

10. Close all the windows.

►**ACTIVITY**

1. Open the **My Computer** window.

2. Start the **Notepad**.

3. Tile the windows vertically. Your screen should appear similar to Figure 2-15.

4. Cascade the windows.

5. Tile the windows horizontally.

6. Click in the **Notepad** window.

7. Exit the **Notepad**.

8. Close the **My Computer** window.

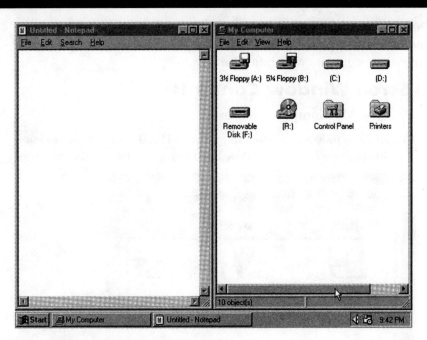

Figure 2-15 These windows are tiled vertically.

# LESSON 21

**Scrolling**

In this lesson, you will learn how to scroll the contents of windows.

## ►SKILL PRACTICE

When a window has more contents than can be displayed in the window at its current size, scroll bars appear, allowing you to *scroll*, or move the contents within the window.

### To Scroll Window Contents

1.  Open the **My Computer** window.

2.  Resize the window as shown in Figure 2-16. At least one scroll bar should appear when the window becomes too small for the contents.

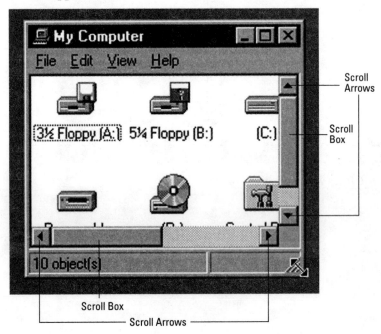

Figure 2-16 Scroll bars appear when a window is too small to display all of its contents.

3.  Click one of the scroll arrows to scroll the contents slightly.

4.  Drag one of the scroll boxes from one end of the scroll bar and then to the other.

5.  Resize the window to make it large enough so that the scroll bars disappear.

6.  Close the window.

GLOSSARY TERMS

SCROLL BARS • graphic elements which allow you to scroll the contents of a window.

LESSON

**21**

►**ACTIVITY**

1. Open the **My Computer** window.

2. Open the **Control Panel** folder in the My Computer window.

3. Resize the **Control Panel** window until the vertical and horizontal scroll bars appear.

4. Practice using the scroll bars to view the contents of the window.

5. Resize the **Control Panel** window to its original size.

6. Close both windows.

# UNIT 2

# Reinforcement Exercise

1. Open the **Recycle Bin** window.

2. Open the **My Computer** window.

3. Switch to the **Recycle Bin** window using the taskbar.

4. Switch to the **My Computer** window by clicking in the My Computer window. Move the Recycle Bin window if necessary.

5. Maximize the **My Computer** window.

6. Switch to the **Recycle Bin** window using the taskbar.

7. Minimize the **Recycle Bin** window.

8. Restore the **My Computer** window.

9. Move the **My Computer** window to a the lower right corner of the screen.

10. Move the **My Computer** window back to its original position.

11. Resize the **My Computer** window to the smallest possible size.

12. Expand the **My Computer** window to be about 2 inches square.

13. Scroll the contents of the **My Computer** window to the left by clicking the right scroll arrow.

14. Resize the **My Computer** window to a size that accommodates all its contents. You may have to scroll back to the left to display all the icons.

15. Redisplay the **Recycle Bin** window.

16. Tile the windows vertically.

17. Cascade the windows.

18. Tile the windows horizontally.

19. Start the **Calculator**.

20. Cascade the windows.

21. Close the **Calculator** and the other windows.

# Challenge Exercise

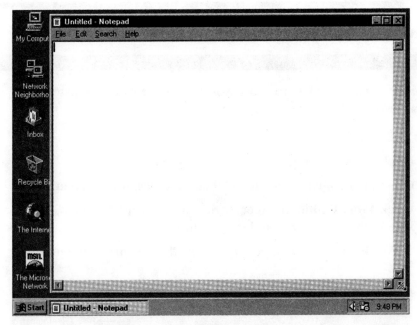

Figure 2-17 You can move and resize a window to occupy whatever area you choose.

1. Start the **Notepad**.
2. Resize and move the **Notepad** to appear as shown in Figure 2-17.
3. Maximize the **Notepad**.
4. Minimize the **Notepad**.
5. Open the **My Computer** window.
6. Redisplay the **Notepad**.
7. Restore the **Notepad**.
8. Cascade the windows.
9. Close the **My Computer** window.
10. Exit the **Notepad**.

# LESSON 22

**Starting WordPad**

In this lesson, you will learn how to start WordPad.

## ►SKILL PRACTICE

WordPad is a simple word processor that can be used to create basic documents such as letters and reports.

### To Start WordPad

1.  Click the **Start** button.

2.  Open the **Programs** menu and then the **Accessories** menu.

3.  Click **WordPad** in the Accessories menu. WordPad starts. Your screen should appear similar to Figure 3-1.

4.  If WordPad does not appear maximized, maximize the window.

<div class="tip">
**TIP** If your screen does not include the toolbar, format bar, or ruler, you can activate them from the View menu. You will learn how to show and hide these screen elements in Lesson 29.
</div>

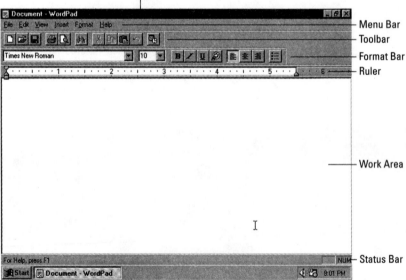

Figure 3-1 WordPad

Title bar - provides the name of the current document
Menu bar - provides the commands available in WordPad
Toolbar - contains icons that provide shortcuts to WordPad commands
Format bar - contains shortcuts for formatting text
Ruler - used to set indents and margins
Work area - area where the document is entered and displayed
Status bar - provides information about the current command

*(continued on next page)*

## ►ACTIVITY

1. Briefly describe the steps required to start WordPad.

2. What is the purpose of the ruler?

3. What is the purpose of the toolbar?

4. In what portion of the WordPad window does the document appear?

5. Where does the document name appear?

***Skill Practice*** *(continued)*

5. Familiarize yourself with the parts of the WordPad screen as identified in Figure 3-1.

6. Leave WordPad open for the lessons that follow.

## ►SKILL PRACTICE

## Dialog Boxes

A dialog box provides information to the user or asks the user to supply more information. A dialog box is a lot like other windows except it contains controls that allow you to communicate with the program. Figure 3-2 shows the features of a typical dialog box.

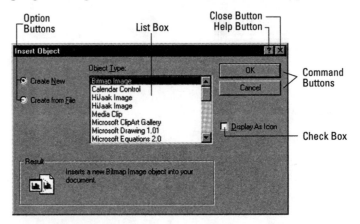

Figure 3-2 A Dialog Box

Dialog boxes can have several kinds of controls. The most common are command buttons, check boxes, option buttons, list boxes, and text boxes.

*Command buttons* are buttons that carry out a command when clicked. Many dialog boxes have OK and Cancel buttons. *Check boxes* allow you to select one or more of a group of options. A check mark or X appears when the option is activated. *Option buttons* allow you to choose only one of a group of options. Only one option in the group can be active at a time. A *list box* allows you to choose an item from a scrolling list. A *text box* allows you to key text in response to a question the dialog box is asking.

Most dialog boxes include some common controls, such as a Close button and a Help button. Click the Help button and then click one of the controls in the dialog box for an explanation.

## GLOSSARY TERMS

DIALOG BOX • a window which provides information to the user or asks the user to supply more information.

COMMAND BUTTONS • buttons which carry out commands.

CHECK BOX • a dialog box control which allows you to choose one or more of a group of options.

OPTION BUTTONS • a dialog box control which allows you to choose only one of a group of options.

LESSON

# 23

## ►ACTIVITY

1. What makes a dialog box different from other windows?

2. What are the most common dialog box controls?

3. How does a check box differ from an Option button?

4. What type of control allows you to choose an item from a scrolling list?

5. Describe how to use the Help button in a dialog box.

**MORE GLOSSARY** TERMS

LIST BOX • a dialog box control which allows you to choose an item from a scrolling list.

TEXT BOX • a dialog box control which allows you to key text in response to a question.

## LESSON

# 24

**Opening a Document**

In this lesson, you will learn how to open a document.

---

## ►SKILL PRACTICE

---

### To Open a Document

Before beginning the steps below, make sure WordPad is running and active on your screen.

1. Place your work disk in the appropriate floppy disk drive.

2. Choose **Open** from the **File** menu. The Open dialog box appears.

3. Click the **down arrow** in the Look In drop down list box, as shown in Figure 3-3.

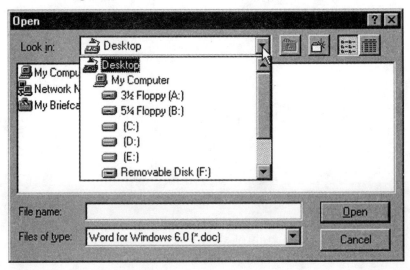

Figure 3-3 The Open Dialog Box

4. Choose the item that identifies the floppy disk drive that holds your work disk. You may need to scroll up or down the list. The files and folders on the work disk appear in the Open dialog box.

5. Click on the document named **United Nations**.

6. Click the **Open** button. The United Nations document opens.

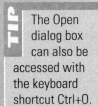
**TIP** The Open dialog box can also be accessed with the keyboard shortcut Ctrl+O.

**NOTE** If your work disk files are on hard disk or a network, your instructor may need to help you locate the files.

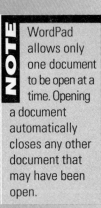
**NOTE** WordPad allows only one document to be open at a time. Opening a document automatically closes any other document that may have been open.

**►ACTIVITY**

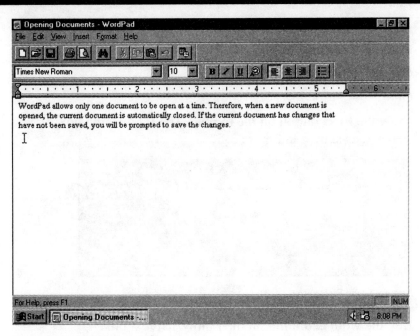

Figure 3-4 An Open Document

1. Open the document named **Opening Documents** from your work disk. The United Nations document closes and the new document appears, as shown in Figure 3-4.

2. Open the **United Nations** document again.

## ►SKILL PRACTICE

**TIP**

To find out the function of a toolbar button, place the pointer on the button and wait for about a second. The name of the button (called a tool tip) appears.

**NOTE**

The Find dialog box offers two search options. The Match Whole Word Only option prevents Find from finding words that are parts of other words. The Match Case option finds only words that match the entered capitalization exactly.

**TIP**

The Enter key can be used to choose the Find Next button.

### To Find Text in a Document

1. Open the **United Nations** document if it is not already open.

2. Choose **Find** from the **Edit** menu.

   Or

   Click the **Find** button on the toolbar. The Find dialog box appears, as shown in Figure 3-5.

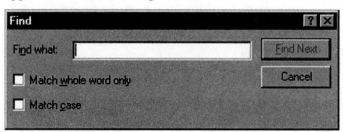

Figure 3-5 Find Dialog Box

3. Key the word **economic** in the Find What text box.

4. Click the **Find Next** button. The first occurrence of the word *economic* appears highlighted.

5. Click **Find Next** repeatedly until WordPad has finished searching the document.

6. Click **OK** to dismiss the message from WordPad.

7. Click **Cancel** to close the Find dialog box.

► **ACTIVITY**

1.  Use the **Find** command to find each occurrence of the word *peace*.

2.  Use the **Find** command to find each occurrence of the compound word *United Nations*.

# LESSON 26

**Using Replace**

In this lesson, you will learn to use the Replace command.

## ►SKILL PRACTICE

### To Find and Replace

WordPad should be running with the United Nations document open.

1.  Choose **Replace** from the **Edit** menu. The Replace dialog box appears.

2.  Key **U.N.** in the Find What text box and press **Tab**. The cursor advances to the next field in the Replace dialog box.

3.  Key **United Nations** in the Replace With text box, as shown in Figure 3-6.

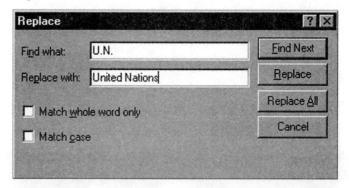

Figure 3-6 Replace Dialog Box

4.  Click the **Find Next** button. The first occurrence of *U.N.* is highlighted.

5.  Click the **Replace** button. The first occurrence of *U.N.* is replaced by *United Nations*. The next occurrence of *U.N.* is automatically located.

6.  Click **Replace**. The second occurrence is replaced, and the third occurrence is found.

7.  Click **Replace All**. The remaining occurrences are replaced.

8.  Click **OK** to dismiss the message box.

9.  Click **Close** to close the Replace dialog box.

# 26

1. Use **Find** to find each occurrence of the word *world*.

2. Use **Replace** to replace all occurrences of *U.S.* with *United States*.

# UNIT 3

# LESSON 27

**Using Page Setup**

In this lesson, you will learn to use the Page Setup command.

## ►SKILL PRACTICE

The Page Setup command allows you to choose paper size, page orientation, and page *margins*.

### To Use Page Setup

WordPad should be open with the United Nations document open.

1. Choose **Page Setup** from the **File** menu. The Page Setup dialog box appears, as shown in Figure 3-7.

> **NOTE**
> The contents of the Page Setup dialog box will vary, depending on the current program and selected printer.

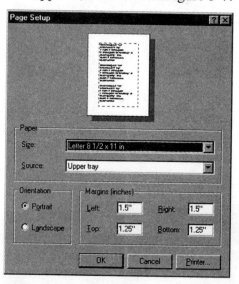

Figure 3-7 Page Setup Dialog Box

2. Click the *Portrait orientation* option if it is not already selected.

3. Press **Tab** repeatedly until the highlight appears in the Left margin text box.

4. Key **1.5** and press **Tab**.

*(continued on next page)*

## GLOSSARY TERMS

MARGIN • the space between the edge of the page and the printed text.

PORTRAIT ORIENTATION • printing text upright on the page, in the normal reading position.

## ►ACTIVITY

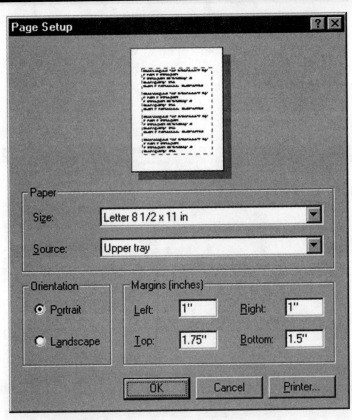

Figure 3-8 New Margins

1. Use **Page Setup** to set the margins of the United Nations document as follows:

   Left Margin: **1"**

   Right Margin: **1"**

   Top Margin: **1.75"**

   Bottom Margin: **1.5"**

2. Compare the Page Setup dialog box on your screen with Figure 3-8.

3. Click **OK** to apply the new margins to your document. The dialog box will close.

---

### *Skill Practice* (continued)

5. Key **1.5** in the Right margin text box and press **Tab**. Notice that the margins of the sample page in the dialog box change as you enter new values.

6. Key **1.5** in the Top margin text box and press **Tab**.

7. Key **2** in the Bottom margin text box.

8. Click **OK** to close the dialog box and apply the new settings to the document.

TIP

Pressing Tab highlights the text in the next text box. When you key new text, the existing text is replaced.

**Printing a Document**

In this lesson, you will learn to print a document.

## ►SKILL PRACTICE

## To Print a Document

1. With the United Nations document open in WordPad, choose **Print** from the **File** menu. The Print dialog box appears, as shown in Figure 3-9. Your Print dialog box may vary slightly from the one in Figure 3-9.

2. Click **OK**. The document prints.

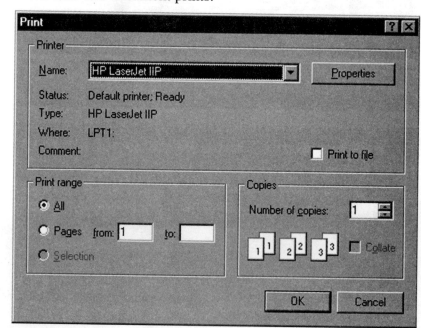

Figure 3-9 Print Dialog Box

## ►ACTIVITY

1. Choose **Print** from the **File** menu.

2. Specify to print only page 2. (Hint: Click the Pages option and enter from 2 to 2 as the range.)

3. Print the page.

UNIT 3

LESSON

29

Changing Settings
in WordPad

In this lesson, you will learn to
change settings in WordPad.

► **SKILL PRACTICE**

## To Show or Hide Screen Elements

1. With the United Nations document open in WordPad, pull down the **View** menu. Notice that the first four items on the menu have check marks by them. These are the currently visible screen elements.

2. Choose **Format Bar**. The check mark disappears and the format bar is hidden.

3. Choose **Ruler** from the **View** menu. The check mark disappears and the ruler is hidden.

4. Choose **Format Bar** from the **View** menu. The check mark reappears, and the format bar is shown again.

5. Choose **Ruler** from the **View** menu. The check mark reappears, and the ruler is shown again.

## To Change the Unit of Measurement

6. Choose **Options** from the **View** menu. The Options dialog box appears. The various sections of the dialog box are accessible by clicking the tabs near the top of the dialog box.

7. Click the **Options** tab. The Options section of the dialog box appears.

8. Click the **Centimeters** measurement unit option button.

9. Click **OK**. Notice the ruler now shows centimeters rather than inches.

10. Choose **Options** from the **View** menu.

11. Click the **Options** tab.

12. Change the measurement unit back to inches and click **OK**.

## LESSON

# 29

## ►ACTIVITY

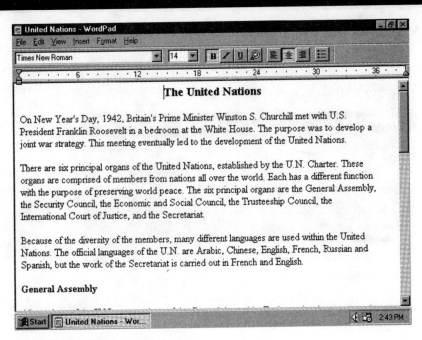

Figure 3-10 The ruler measures in picas.

1. Hide the **toolbar**.

2. Hide the **status bar**.

3. Change the measurement units to *picas*. The screen appears as shown in Figure 3-10.

4. Change the measurement units to *points*.

5. Change the measurement units back to inches.

6. Show the **toolbar** and **status bar**.

UNIT 3

LESSON

# 30

**Closing a Document and Exiting WordPad**

In this lesson, you will learn to close a document and exit WordPad.

## ►SKILL PRACTICE

### To Close a Document and Exit WordPad

1. With the United Nations document open in WordPad, choose **Exit** from the **File** menu. WordPad will ask if you want to save changes to the document.

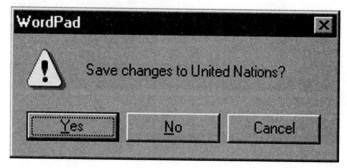

Figure 3-11 Save Changes Dialog Box

2. Click **No**. WordPad closes, and you are returned to the Windows desktop.

## ACTIVITY

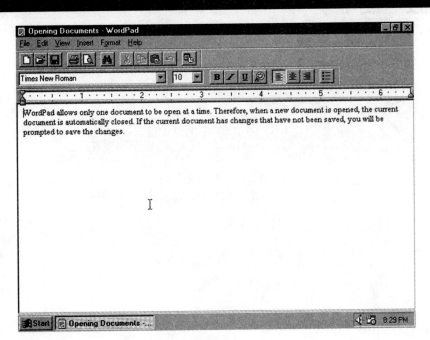

Figure 3-12 WordPad with an Open Document

# UNIT 3

# Reinforcement Exercise

1. Start **WordPad**.

2. Open the document named **Letter of Application** from your work disk.

3. Use **Replace** to replace the word *service* with *construction*.

4. Use **Page Setup** to set the left and right margins to 1.75 inches and the top margin to 2 inches. Leave the bottom margin unchanged.

5. Print the document.

6. Exit **WordPad** without saving.

# Challenge Exercise

**GLOSSARY** TERMS

LANDSCAPE ORIENTATION • printing text sideways on the page.

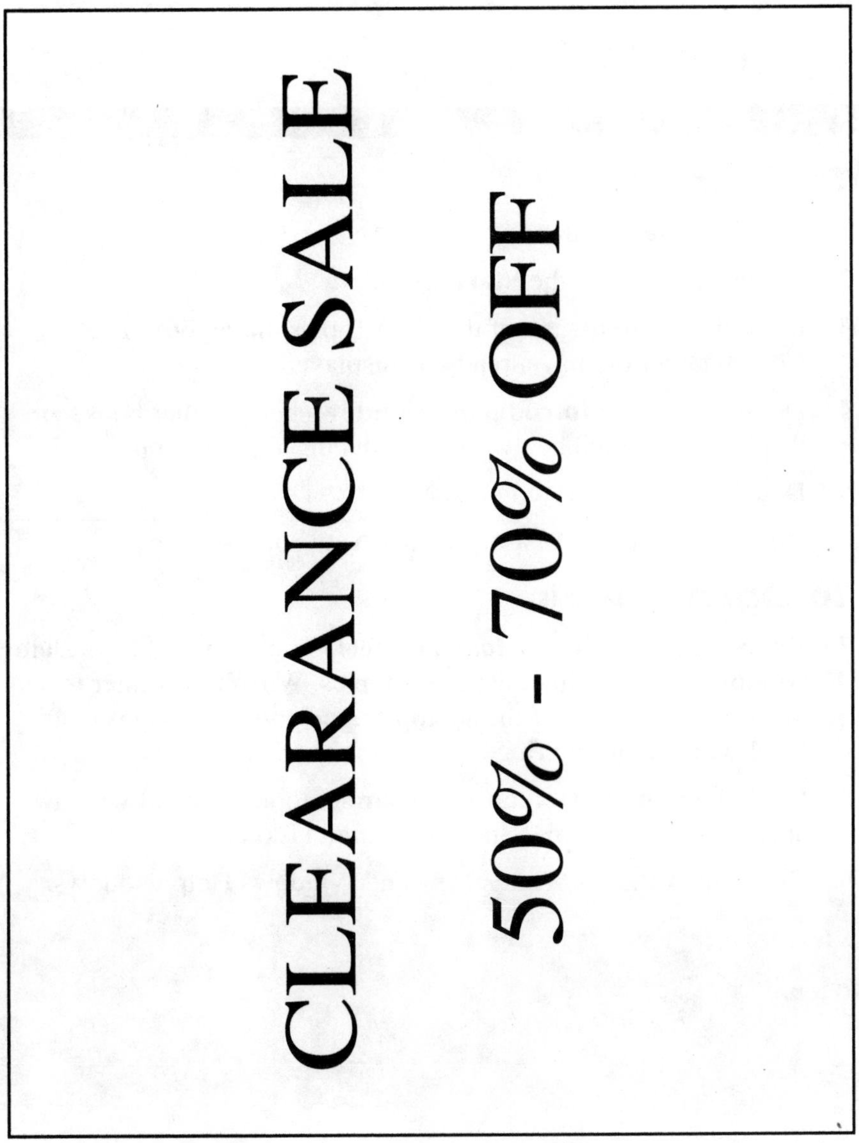


**Figure 3-13 Landscape Orientation**

1. Start **WordPad**.
2. Open the document named **Poster** from your work disk.
3. Use **Page Setup** to set the document to print in *landscape orientation*.
4. Set the left and right margins to 1 inch.
5. Print the document. The printout should appear similar to Figure 3-13.
6. Exit **WordPad** without saving.

# LESSON 31

**Using Help Topics by Contents**

In this lesson, you will learn to look up Windows Help topics by contents.

## ►SKILL PRACTICE

**NOTE**

Help topics are grouped into categories called *books*. Books are indicated by a small book icon. Topics are indicated by an icon with a question mark (?) on it.

**TIP**

After opening a Help topic, return to the Contents by clicking the Help Topics button in the Windows Help window. The open Help windows, however, do not close when you return to the Contents.

### To Open a Book

1. Click the **Start** button.

2. Choose **Help** from the **Start** menu.

3. Click the **Contents** tab of the Help Topics dialog box. The Contents section may already be displayed.

4. Double-click the **Introducing Windows** book. Other books are displayed indented below the Introducing Windows book.

5. Double-click the **Welcome** book.

6. Double-click the **A List of What's New** book.

### To Open a Topic

7. Double-click the **A new look and feel** topic. The Windows Help window appears with a list of subtopics. When the pointer is positioned over one of the subtopics, the pointer changes to a hand with a pointing finger.

8. Click the **Start button and taskbar** subtopic. A small window appears, discussing the Start button and taskbar.

9. Close the A List of What's New and Windows Help windows.

GLOSSARY TERMS

BOOK • a category of Help topics

## ►ACTIVITY

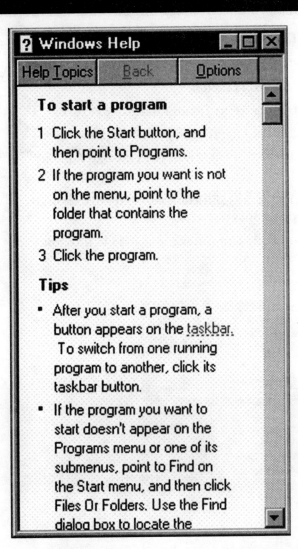

**To start a program**

1 Click the Start button, and then point to Programs.

2 If the program you want is not on the menu, point to the folder that contains the program.

3 Click the program.

**Tips**

- After you start a program, a button appears on the taskbar. To switch from one running program to another, click its taskbar button.

- If the program you want to start doesn't appear on the Programs menu or one of its submenus, point to Find on the Start menu, and then click Files Or Folders. Use the Find dialog box to locate the

Figure 4-1 Windows Help

1. Access the Help Contents.

2. Open the **How To...** book.

3. Open the **Run Programs** book.

4. Open the **Starting a program** topic. The Windows Help window appears, as shown in Figure 4-1.

5. Close the Help window.

**Using Help Topics by
Index**

In this lesson, you will learn to use
Windows Help topics by index.

## ►SKILL PRACTICE

### To Access Help Topics by Index

1. Click the **Start** button.

2. Choose **Help** from the **Start** menu.

3. Click the **Index** tab of the Help Topics dialog box.

4. Key **r**. The index moves to the first entry that begins with *r*.

5. Key **est** following the *r*. The index moves to the entry about
   restarting, as shown in Figure 4-2.

6. Click the entry for restarting your computer and click **Display**.
   A list of several topics appears.

7. Click the **Restarting your computer** topic and click **Display**
   again. Help on restarting your computer appears.

8. Close the **Windows Help** window.

> **NOTE**
> As you key
> text in the
> Index section
> of the Help
> Topics dialog
> box, the index
> advances to the
> nearest match to
> what you have
> keyed.

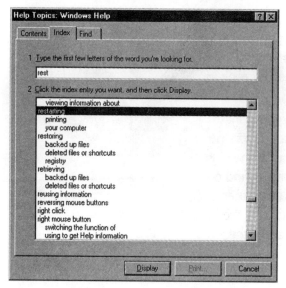

Figure 4-2 Help by Index

## ►ACTIVITY

1. Access the Help Topics index.

2. Search for help on minimizing windows. Read and close the Help window.

3. Search for help on cascading windows. The Windows Help window appears as shown in Figure 4-3.

4. Close the Windows Help window.

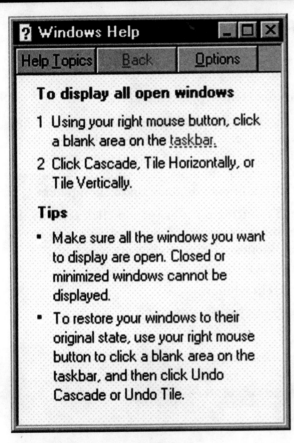

**Figure 4-3 Help on Cascading Windows**

LESSON
# 33

**Using Find**

## ►SKILL PRACTICE

## To Access Help Topics Using Find

1. Click the **Start** button.

2. Choose **Help** from the Start menu.

3. Click the **Find** tab of the Help Topics dialog box.

4. Key **exit**. The Find feature is case sensitive, meaning that keying the text for which you are searching in all caps will prevent the Find feature from finding the topic. Topics appear near the bottom of the dialog box. Your screen should appear similar to Figure 4-4. The number of topics found will vary among computers.

5. Click the topic named **Quitting a program** and click **Display**. If your screen includes more topics than Figure 4-4, you may have to scroll the list. The Windows Help window appears with information on quitting a program.

6. Close the **Windows Help** window.

**TIP**

You can also double-click a topic to display it without clicking the Display button.

**NOTE**

The first time you access the Find section of the Help Topics dialog box, you must allow Windows to set up the Find word list. Use the setup recommended by the Find Setup Wizard.

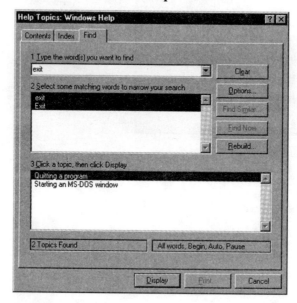

Figure 4-4 Using Find

---

## ►ACTIVITY

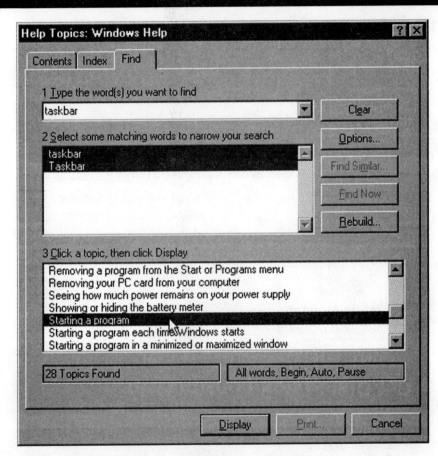

Figure 4-5 Find has located more than 20 topics.

1. Use Find to find help on the taskbar.

2. Choose the help topic on Starting a program, as shown in Figure 4-5. You must scroll the list of topics.

3. Display the Help topic.

4. Close the Windows Help window.

# LESSON 34

**Printing Help Topics**

In this lesson, you will print Help topics.

## ▶SKILL PRACTICE

### To Print from the Windows Help Window

1. Choose **Help** from the Start menu.
2. Click the **Contents** tab of the Help Topics dialog box.
3. Open the **How To...** book.
4. Open the **Use Help** book.
5. Open the **Copying information from a Help topic** topic.
6. Click the **Options** button. A menu appears, as shown in Figure 4-6.
7. Choose **Print Topic** from the menu. The Print dialog box appears.
8. Click **OK**. The topic prints.

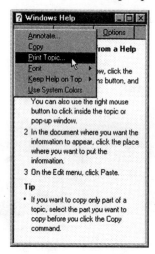

Figure 4-6 The Options Menu

### To Print from the Contents Section of the Help Topics Dialog Box

9. Click the **Help Topics** button to return to the Help Topics dialog box.
10. Click the topic **Printing a Help topic**.
11. Click the **Print** button. The Print dialog box appears.
12. Click **OK**.
13. Close the Help window.

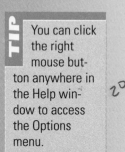

**TIP** You can click the right mouse button anywhere in the Help window to access the Options menu.

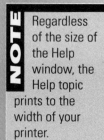

**NOTE** Regardless of the size of the Help window, the Help topic prints to the width of your printer.

**TIP** Clicking on a book and choosing Print will print all the topics in the book.

## ►ACTIVITY

1. Use the index to find help on resizing windows. Open the topic that covers the basics.

2. Print the topic.

3. Close the Help window.

## ►SKILL PRACTICE

Annotating a Help topic allows you to add a note or additional information to the topic.

### To Annotate a Help Topic

1.  Choose **Help** from the Start menu.

2.  Use the index to find and open the topic on switching between windows. Open the topic called **Switching between running programs**.

3.  Click the **Options** button. The Options menu appears.

4.  Choose **Annotate** from the menu. A small window appears to allow you to enter the annotation.

5.  Enter the annotation shown in Figure 4-7.

6.  Click **Save**.

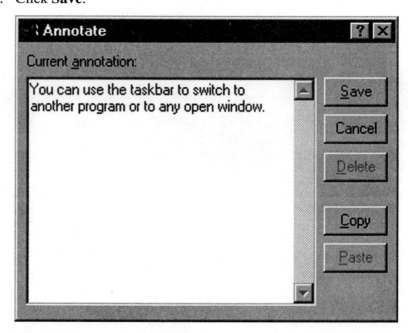

Figure 4-7 You can annotate any Help topic.

*(continued on next page)*

LESSON

# 35

## ►ACTIVITY

*Skill Practice (continued)*

## To Read an Annotation

Once you have annotated a Help topic, Windows indicates the annotation by marking the topic with a paper clip. Figure 4-8 shows the paper clip icon, which indicates that an annotation has been attached to the topic.

Paper Clip Icon

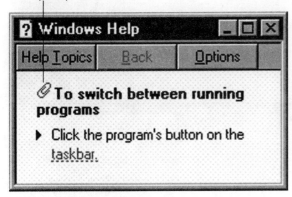

Figure 4-8 Clicking the paper clip opens the annotation.

7. Click the **paper clip**.

8. Read the annotation and click **Cancel**.

9. Close the Help window.

1. Use the index to find and open the Help topic on annotation.

2. Add the following note by using the Annotate command.

   **Annotation allows you to add information to a Help topic.**

3. Use the index to find and open the Help topic on switching between windows.

4. Read the annotation attached to that topic.

5. Click the **Delete** button to delete the annotation.

6. Find the topic about the Annotate command again.

7. Read and delete the annotation attached to the Annotate topic.

8. Close the Help window.

**TIP**
You can delete an annotation by clicking its paper clip and clicking the Delete button in the Annotation window.

LESSON

# 36

**Positioning Help Windows**

In this lesson, you will learn how to position help windows in relation to other programs.

## ▶SKILL PRACTICE

**TIP**

You may want to keep Help on top when you are following step-by-step instructions from a Help window.

You can choose to always keep Help windows on top of other programs which are running.

### To Keep Help Windows on Top

1. Use the index to find and open the topic on switching between running programs.
2. Click the **Options** button. The Options menu appears.
3. Choose **Keep Help on Top** from the menu. A submenu appears.
4. Choose **On Top** from the submenu.
5. Open **WordPad**. Notice the Windows Help window stays on top (see Figure 4-9).

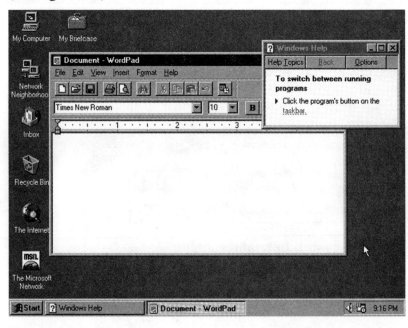

Figure 4-9 Keeping Help windows on top ensures that the Help information will always be visible.

### To Keep Help Windows in Back

6. Click the **Options** button in the Windows Help window.
7. Choose **Keep Help on Top**.

*(continued on next page)*

## ►ACTIVITY

1. Open **WordPad**.

2. Using the Help index, look up Help and open the Help topic on keeping Help in front of other windows.

3. Set the Help window to always be on top.

4. Switch to **WordPad**. Notice the Help window.

5. Switch to the Help window.

6. Set the Help window not to be on top.

7. Switch to **WordPad**. The Help window does not appear.

8. Use the taskbar to access the Help window.

9. Set the Help window to the default window position.

10. Exit **WordPad** and close **Help**.

***Skill Practice*** *(continued)*

8. Choose **Not On Top** from the submenu.

9. Click on the **WordPad** work area to make it active. The Help window is covered by WordPad.

10. Click **Windows Help** in the taskbar. The Help window is brought back to the top.

## To Return to the Default Setting

11. Click the **Options** button in the Windows Help window.

12. Choose **Keep Help on Top**.

13. Choose **Default**.

14. Switch to **WordPad**.

15. Exit **WordPad**.

16. Close the Help window.

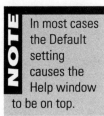

**NOTE** In most cases the Default setting causes the Help window to be on top.

LESSON

# 37

**Help with Button Names**

In this lesson, you will learn how to get help identifying toolbar buttons.

## ►SKILL PRACTICE

### To Identify the Name of a Button

1. Start **WordPad**.

2. Position the pointer over the first button on the left end of the toolbar (the New button). After a short pause, the name of the button appears.

3. Position the pointer on other buttons on the toolbar.

4. Position the pointer on the Bold button on the Format bar, as shown in Figure 4-10.

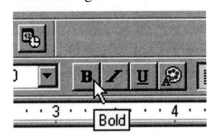

Figure 4-10 Resting the pointer on a button displays the button's name.

### To Display the Full Name of a Taskbar Button

5. Minimize **WordPad**.

6. Open the **My Computer** window and the **Recycle Bin** window.

7. Switch to the **My Computer** window and open the **Control Panel** folder.

8. Position the pointer on the **WordPad** taskbar button. The full name of the task appears.

9. Exit **WordPad**.

10. Close the **My Computer** and the **Recycle Bin** windows.

►**ACTIVITY**

1.  Start **WordPad**.
2.  Rest the pointer on the buttons of the toolbar and Format bar one at a time. Write the name of the button next to its icon.
3.  Exit **WordPad**.

a. _____

b. _____

c. _____

d. _____

e. _____

f. _____

g. _____

h. _____

i. _____

j. _____

# UNIT 4

## LESSON

# 38

**Help with Menu Commands**

In this lesson, you will learn how to get help identifying menu commands.

---

## ►SKILL PRACTICE

**TIP** If the Status Bar is not visible, choose Status Bar from the View menu.

Additional information about menu commands is provided in the status bar.

## To Get Help Identifying Menu Commands

1. Start **WordPad**.

2. Pull down the **Insert** menu.

3. Move the pointer to the **Date and Time** command. A brief description of the command appears in the status bar, as shown in Figure 4-11.

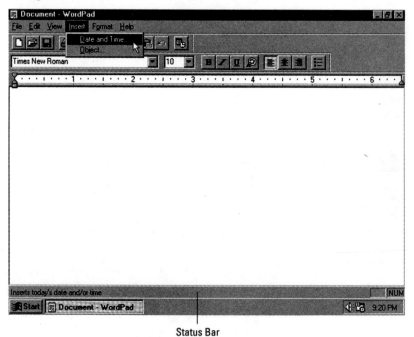

Status Bar

Figure 4-11 The status bar describes commands.

## ►ACTIVITY

New _____

Open _____

Save _____

Save As _____

Exit _____

1. With WordPad open, pull down the **File** menu.

2. Beside each of the command names, write the descriptive line that appears in the status bar when the pointer rests on the command.

3. Exit **WordPad**.

# LESSON 39

**Dialog Box Help**

In this lesson, you will learn how to get help with dialog box controls.

## ►SKILL PRACTICE

### To Get Dialog Box Control Help

1. Start **WordPad**.

2. Choose **Print** from the **File** menu. The Print dialog box appears.

3. Click the **Help** button in the Print dialog box, as shown in Figure 4-12. A question mark (?) is added to the pointer.

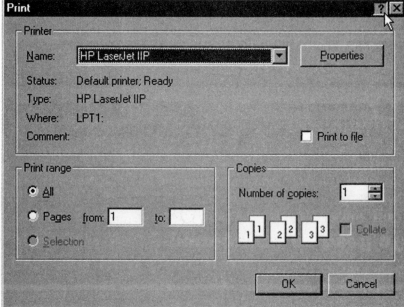

Help Button

Figure 4-12 The Help Button

4. Click inside the **Number of copies** text box. A brief explanation of the use of the control appears in a pop-up window.

5. Click the pop-up window. The window closes.

6. Click the **Help** button again.

7. Click the **Cancel** button. A description of what the Cancel button does appears in a pop-up window.

8. Click the pop-up window.

9. Click **Cancel** to close the dialog box.

►**ACTIVITY**

1. Choose **Page Setup** from the **File** menu.

2. In the blanks provided, write the text provided in the Help button pop-up window for that area.

3. Close the **Page Setup** dialog box and exit **WordPad**.

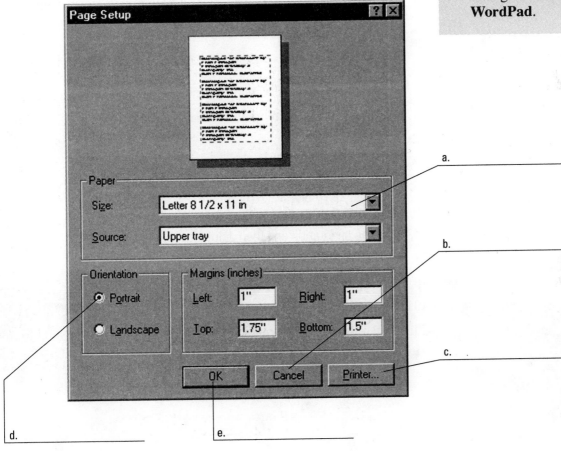

Figure 4-13

# UNIT 4

# Reinforcement Exercise

1. Start **Help** and go to the **Contents** tab.
2. Open the **Tips and Tricks** book.
3. Open the **Tips of the Day** book.
4. Open a topic that interests you.
5. Read the topic and then return to Help Topics.
6. Switch to the **Index** tab and look up **Help**.
7. Read the topic under Help named **Tips for using**. Your version of Help may have a slightly different name for the topic, such as Tips: Using Help.
8. Close the **Help** window.
9. Start **Help** again.
10. Use **Find** to locate topics relating to software piracy.
11. Open the topic called **What is software piracy?**
12. Print the topic.
13. Annotate the topic with any text you choose.
14. Close the **Help** window.
15. Use the Help index to find the topic you annotated.
16. Read the annotation and then delete it.
17. Close the **Help** window.
18. Start the **NotePad**.
19. Choose **Find** from the **Search** menu.
20. Use the **Help** button to get an explanation of the Direction control.
21. Cancel the dialog box and exit the **NotePad**.

# Challenge Exercise

1. Open the **My Computer** window and the **Recycle Bin** window.

2. Start **WordPad**, the **Calculator**, and the **NotePad**.

3. Start **Help** and use the Index to find and open the topic on copyright infringement.

4. While the topic is displayed, set the option that keeps Help on top.

5. Switch to **WordPad**.

6. Access the **Open** dialog box. You may have to resize the Help window to be able to see the entire Open dialog box.

7. Use dialog box help to get an explanation of the File name text box.

8. Open the document called **Letter of Application** from your work disk.

9. Switch to the **Calculator**.

10. Switch back to **WordPad**.

11. Position the pointer over several toolbar buttons to display button names.

12. Position the pointer on each of the taskbar buttons long enough to display the entire button name.

13. Make the Help window active and change the **Keep Help on Top** setting back to the default.

14. Close the **Help** window.

15. Exit the programs that are running and close all windows.

**Creating a New Document**

In this lesson, you will learn how to create a new document and how to key text.

## ►SKILL PRACTICE

### To Start WordPad and Begin a Document

1. Start **WordPad**. Opening WordPad automatically creates a new document.

2. Enter the following text with the keyboard:

   **You can create a new document in WordPad by simply keying text after WordPad starts.**

### To Create a New Document

**TIP** If you make a mistake, you can use the Backspace key to delete the character you just typed.

3. Choose **New** from the **File** menu.

   Or

   Click the **New** button on the toolbar.

   The New dialog box appears, as shown in Figure 5-1, asking what type of document you want.

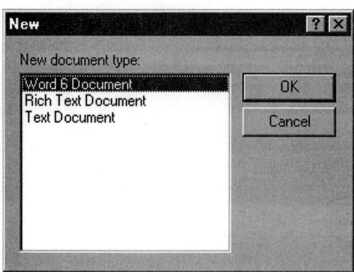

Figure 5-1 New Dialog Box

4. Choose **Word 6 Document** and click **OK**. A message box appears, asking if you want to save the current document.

5. Click **No**. A new document appears.

**TIP** You can access the New command by pressing Ctrl+N.

## ► ACTIVITY

Have you ever wondered what you would do if you could change your past? Maybe you wish you could have hit a home run in the Little League championships instead of striking out. We all think about it at some time or another. The present is a time to think about the future and learn from the past. The future is not etched in stone, so try to make the best of it.

1. Enter the following sentences into a new WordPad document.

   **To create a new document, choose New from the File menu. You will be prompted to save the current document.**

2. Create a new document without saving the current document and key in the paragraph at left.

3. Print the document.

4. Exit **WordPad** without saving the new document.

# LESSON 41

**Selecting Text**

In this lesson, you will learn how to select text in a document.

## ►SKILL PRACTICE

Before performing an operation on text, you must select the text which you want to effect.

### To Select a Word

To *select* one word, you can double-click on the word you wish to select.

1. Start **WordPad**.

2. Choose **Open** from the **File** menu.

   Or

    Click the **Open** button in the toolbar.

3. Open the document named **The Internet** from your work disk.

4. Position the pointer on the word **institutions** in the first paragraph and double-click. The word *institutions* is selected.

### To Select an Entire Paragraph

To select a paragraph, you can triple-click anywhere in the paragraph you wish to select.

5. Position the pointer anywhere in the first paragraph and triple-click. The paragraph is selected.

### To Select Any Amount of Text

To select any amount of text, click at the beginning of the selection and drag to the end of the text you wish to highlight.

6. Position the pointer at the beginning of the first word of the second paragraph.

7. Drag the pointer to the end of the sentence. The entire sentence is selected.

### To Select All Text

8. Choose **Select All** from the **Edit** menu. The entire document is selected.

9. Click anywhere in the document to deselect the text.

GLOSSARY TERMS
SELECT • to highlight text in order to
perform operations on it.

LESSON
41

# ►ACTIVITY

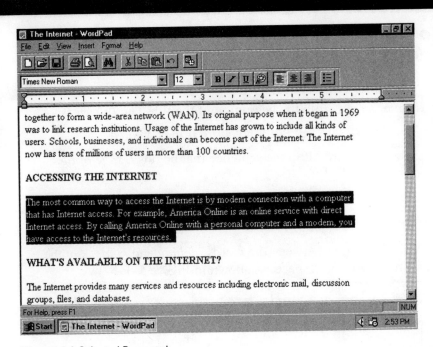

Figure 5-2 A Selected Paragraph

1. If it is not already open, open the document named **The Internet**. Select the acronym **WAN** in the first paragraph.

2. Select the entire paragraph under the heading *Accessing the Internet*. Your screen should look similar to Figure 5-2.

3. Select the entire document except for the first paragraph and the title.

4. Select the entire document.

5. Exit **WordPad**.

UNIT 5

LESSON

42

Editing Text

In this lesson, you will learn how to delete and insert text.

►**SKILL PRACTICE**

**NOTE**

The Delete key erases the character to the right of cursor. The backspace key erases characters to the left of the cursor.

**TIP**

Holding down the Delete key will repeat the delete operation rapidly.

## To Delete Text

1. Start **WordPad**.

2. Open the document named **The Internet**.

3. Move the cursor to the beginning of the title *The Internet*.

4. Press the **Delete** key until the entire title is deleted.

5. Select the word **all** in the sentence that begins *Usage of the Internet*.

6. Press the **Delete** key. The highlighted text is deleted.

## To Insert Text

7. With the cursor between the words *include* and *kinds*, key the word **many** and a space, as shown in Figure 5-3.

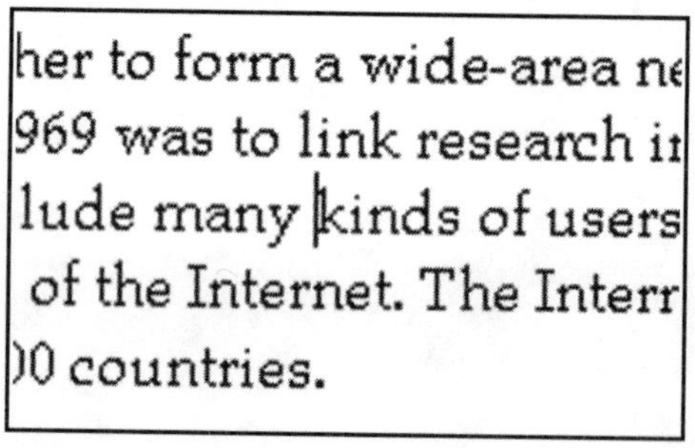

her to form a wide-area ne
969 was to link research in
lude many |kinds of users
 of the Internet. The Interr
)0 countries.

Figure 5-3 Inserting Text

## ►ACTIVITY

```
with each other. The in
user has an electronic n
has an account and the
electronic |mail address
symbol '@'. Following
type of organization. F
the government has the
```

Figure 5-4 Edited Text

1. Delete all the headings in the document.

2. In the paragraph about electronic mail, position the cursor in the sentence that begins *In an e-mail address*.

3. Edit the sentence to begin *In an electronic mail address*, as shown in Figure 5-4.

4. Exit **WordPad** without saving.

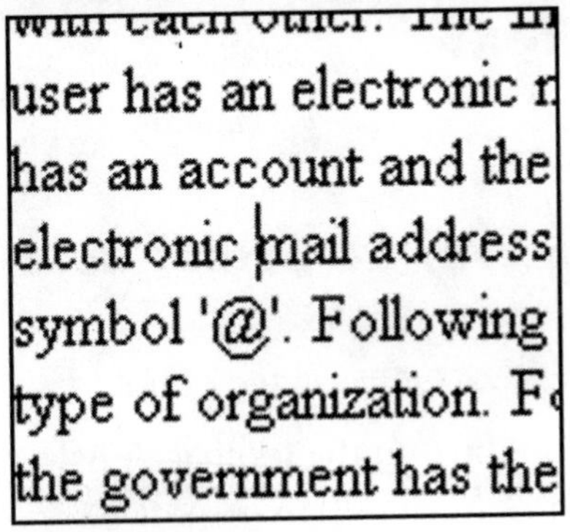

**Applying Fonts, Styles, Colors**

## ►SKILL PRACTICE

### To Change the Font of Text

1. Start **WordPad**.

2. Key the following text:

   **This sentence appears in red, 14-point, bold Courier New font.**

3. Select the entire sentence.

4. Click the arrow at the end of the Font box on the toolbar. A list of *fonts* appears, as shown in Figure 5-5.

5. Choose **Courier New** from the font list. You may need to scroll to find Courier New. The typeface changes.

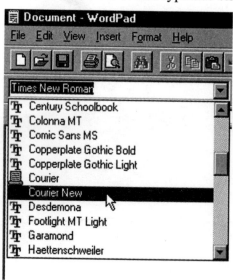

Figure 5-5 The Font Box

6. Be sure the sentence is still selected. Choose **14** from the Size box next to the Font box on the toolbar. The size enlarges to 14 point.

*(continued on next page)*

> **TIP**
> You can set the font, size, *style*, and color for text before you key the text. Just position your cursor where you want the text to appear, choose the font, size, style, and color you want, and begin keying.

> **TIP**
> You can also italicize and underline text from toolbar buttons next to the Bold button.

**GLOSSARY** TERMS

FONT • a typeface or design of type.

STYLE • variations in the appearance of text, such as bolding, underlining, and italics.

LESSON

# 43

## ► ACTIVITY

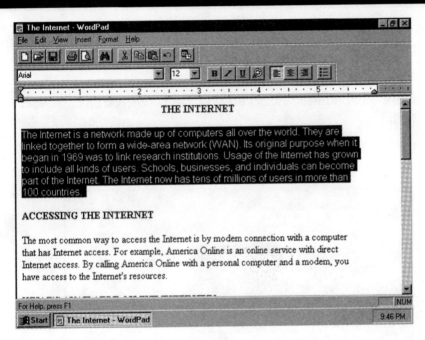

Figure 5-6 Changing Font

1. Open the document named **The Internet**. Do not save the current document.

2. Highlight the title and change the color to blue.

3. Highlight the first paragraph and change the font to Arial. Your screen should appear similar to Figure 5-6.

4. Change the title and the first two headings to 14 point. (Hint: If 14 point does not appear on the size menu, click the size text box and key 14.)

5. Print the document. You will not see the colors in the document unless you have a color printer.

6. Exit **WordPad** without saving.

*Skill Practice* (*continued*)

## To Change the Style of Text

7. Be sure the sentence is still selected. Click on the **Bold** button on the toolbar.

## To Change the Color of Text

8. Be sure the sentence is still selected. Click the **Color** button on the toolbar.

9. Choose **Red** from the menu that appears.

10. Click anywhere in the document to deselect the sentence.

UNIT 5

LESSON

# 44

Formatting Paragraphs

In this lesson, you will learn how to set indentation and align paragraphs.

## ►SKILL PRACTICE

### To Indent Text from the Paragraph Dialog Box

1. Start **WordPad**.

2. Open the Job Interview document from your work disk.

3. Highlight the entire document, except for the title.

4. Choose **Paragraph** from the **Format** menu. The Paragraph dialog box appears, as shown in Figure 5-7.

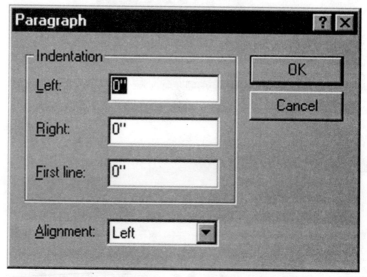

Figure 5-7 Paragraph Dialog Box

5. Press **Tab** twice to place the cursor in the First Line text box. Key **.25**.

6. Click **OK**. The first line of each paragraph is indented $\frac{1}{4}$ inch.

### To Indent Text Using the Ruler

Indents can be changed by dragging the first-line indent marker, the left indent marker, and the right indent marker (see Figure 5-8).

*(continued on next page)*

## ►ACTIVITY

*Skill Practice* (continued)

Left Indent Marker
First Indent Marker
Right Indent Marker

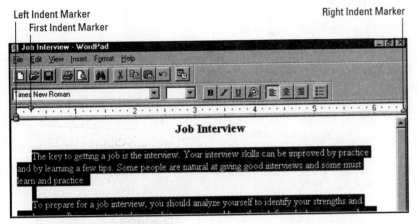

Figure 5-8 Indent Markers

7. With the text still selected, drag the first-line indent marker to the left margin (directly above the left indent marker). The paragraphs are no longer indented.

8. Drag the small rectangle at the base of the left indent marker to the 1-inch mark on the ruler. The left indent marker and first-line indent marker move together.

9. Drag the right indent marker to the 5-inch mark on the ruler.

## To Change Alignment

You can choose a text alignment from the Paragraph dialog box or by clicking an alignment button on the toolbar.

10. Highlight the first paragraph only.

11. Click the **Align Right** button on the toolbar. The paragraph aligns to the right margin.

12. Click the **Center** button on the toolbar. The paragraph is centered.

13. Click the **Align Left** button. The paragraph is returned to left alignment.

14. Print the document.

1. Open **The Internet** document without saving the changes made to the Job Interview document.

2. Highlight the second paragraph.

3. Give the paragraph a first-line indent of 0.25 inch.

4. Give all the paragraphs that follow a first-line indent of 0.25 inch. Leave the first paragraph unindented.

5. Center the first two headings in the body of the document.

6. Change the font size of the document's title to 18 point.

7. Print the document.

8. Exit **WordPad** without saving.

**NOTE** Indentations and alignment apply to the paragraph that the cursor is in or to all highlighted paragraphs.

► **SKILL PRACTICE**

## To Use Undo

1. Start **WordPad**.

2. Enter the following text:

   **The Undo command can reverse the effects of the most recent command or action.**

3. Delete the word *reverse* in the sentence you just keyed.

4. Choose **Undo** from the **Edit** menu. The word is replaced.

5. Highlight the sentence and change the alignment to center.

 6. Click the **Undo** button on the toolbar. The previous alignment is restored.

> **NOTE**
> The Undo button performs the same function as the Undo command on the Edit menu.

## ►ACTIVITY

1. Create a new document without saving the existing one.
2. Key the following sentence:

   **When using computers, many operations essentially do the same thing.**
3. Change the color of the sentence to red.
4. Undo the color change.
5. Undo the color change again to make it red.
6. Delete the sentence.
7. Undo the deletion.
8. Exit **WordPad**.

**Saving a Document**

In this lesson you will learn how to save your documents to a disk.

## ►SKILL PRACTICE

### To Save a Document

Use the Save As command the first time you save a document or if you want to give an existing document a new name. Use the Save command to save changes to a document that has already been named.

1. Start **WordPad**.

2. Enter the following paragraph:

   **In the period between 1910 and 1920, more than 30 million people (about 30% of Americans) lived on farms in the United States. By 1992, only about 2% (about 4.6 million) of the population lived on farms.**

NOTE

The contents of the Save As dialog box on your screen may vary from Figure 5-9.

3. Choose **Save As** from the **File** menu. The Save As dialog box appears, as shown in Figure 5-9.

Figure 5-9 Save As Dialog Box

4. From the **Save In** pop-up list, choose the floppy disk drive that holds your work disk (probably the one labeled A:).

5. Click in the **File Name** text box. The cursor appears in the text box.

6. Delete the existing name and key **Ag Population** as the filename.

*(continued on next page)*

## ►ACTIVITY

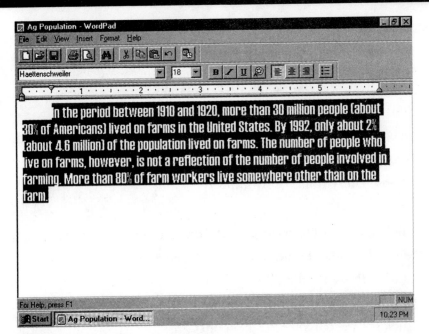

Figure 5-10 Paragraph After Font and Format Changes

1. Change the font of the paragraph to a font of your choice.

2. Set the font size to 18-point.

3. Set a first-line indent of 0.5 inches. Your screen should appear similar to Figure 5-10.

4. Save the document to your work disk as **Ag Population 2**.

5. Print the document and exit **WordPad**.

*Skill Practice (continued)*

7. Click the **Save** button. The document is saved, and the dialog box closes.

8. Add the following sentences to the end of the existing paragraph:

   **The number of people who live on farms, however, is not a reflection of the number of people involved in farming. More than 80% of farm workers live somewhere other than on the farm.**

9. Choose **Save** from the **File** menu.

   Or

   Click the **Save** button on the toolbar.

   The document is saved again.

10. Print the document.

NOTE

Using the Save As command to save a document with a new name actually saves a new copy of the file. The existing document will remain on the disk with the previous name.

**Copying Text**

In this lesson, you will learn how to copy text within a document.

## ►SKILL PRACTICE

### To Copy Text

To copy text within a document, highlight the text you want to copy, choose the Copy command, place the cursor where you want the copy to appear, and choose the Paste command.

1.  Start **WordPad**.

2.  Open the document named **Job Interview**.

3.  Highlight the first sentence.

 4.  Choose **Copy** from the **Edit** menu.

Or

Click the **Copy** button on the toolbar.

5.  Move the cursor to the end of the document.

 6.  Choose **Paste** from the **Edit** menu.

Or

Click the **Paste** button on the toolbar.

**GLOSSARY** TERMS

CLIPBOARD • the area in the computer's memory where text that has been cut or copied is held.

---

►**ACTIVITY**

---

1. Select the first paragraph.
2. Copy the paragraph and paste it at the end of the document.
3. Paste the paragraph at the end of the document again.
4. Exit **WordPad** without saving.

# LESSON
# 48

**Moving Text**

In this lesson, you will learn how to move text within a document.

## ►SKILL PRACTICE

### To Move Text

To move text, highlight the text you want to move, choose the Cut command, position the pointer where you want the text inserted, and choose the Paste command.

1. Start **WordPad** and open the document named **The Internet**.

2. Highlight the heading *ACCESSING THE INTERNET* and the paragraph that follows it. Include the blank line that follows the paragraph.

3. Choose **Cut** from the Edit menu.

   Or

   Click the **Cut** button on the toolbar.

   The selected text is removed.

4. Move the cursor to the end of the document.

5. Press **Enter** to create a blank line.

6. Click the **Paste** button on the toolbar.

**NOTE**

Like the Copy command, the Cut command places text on the Clipboard. The difference is that the Cut command removes the text from its original position.

## ►ACTIVITY

1. Open **The Internet** if it is not already open.
2. Cut the *World Wide Web* heading and the paragraph that follows it.
3. Paste it above the *Electronic Mail* heading.
4. Save the document as **The Internet 2**.
5. Print the document.
6. Exit **WordPad**.

**Saving Documents in Other Formats**

# ►SKILL PRACTICE

## File Formats

WordPad can save documents in four distinct file formats.

- Word for Windows 6.0 format
- Rich Text Format (RTF)
- Text Document
- Text Document—MS-DOS Format

The default file format is Word for Windows 6.0. Word for Windows is a full-featured word processing program from Microsoft. Rich Text Format is a format that allows formatted documents to be transferred from one word processor to another without losing the formatting. Text Document saves only the text on the document, losing any formatting such as bold and italics. The MS-DOS Format should be used when the text will be used by an MS-DOS program, rather than a Windows-based program.

## To Save a Document in a Chosen Format

1. Start **WordPad** and open the document named **The Internet**.
2. Choose **Save As** from the **File** menu.
3. Make sure the Save In box shows the location of your work disk.
4. Click the **Save as Type** list box. The list of formats drops down.
5. Click **Rich Text Format (RTF)**.
6. Name the new document **The Internet (RTF)**.
7. Click **Save**.

> **TIP**
> The ability to save WordPad documents in a variety of formats makes it possible to enter text into WordPad and later import the text into other word processors.

## ►ACTIVITY

**Kim Lee is a freelance computer consultant specializing in networking with Windows. After earning a degree in Computer Science from Simmons Technological College, Kim worked as network specialist for DTK Corporation for 5 years before becoming an independent consultant. Kim's interests include mountain climbing, reading, tennis, and model railroading.**

Figure 5-12

1. Create a new document.

2. Key a short biography of yourself. Give your name, accomplishments, and other information about yourself. Make the paragraph no more than four or five sentences. (See the example in Figure 5-12.)

3. Save the document to your work disk in **Text Document** format by using your name as the filename.

4. Print the document.

5. Exit **WordPad**.

# Reinforcement Exercise

1. Start **WordPad**.
2. Key the text shown at right into a blank document.
3. Select the entire second paragraph.
4. Select the last sentence of the document.
5. Edit the end of the first sentence of the document to read as follows:

   When working with computers, you will often see file sizes and memory sizes referred to using terms like byte, kilobyte, megabyte, gigabyte, and terabyte.

6. Add the following sentence to the end of the last paragraph in the document.

   The next level of storage size, which is becoming more common, is the terabyte (1 trillion bytes).

7. Change the font of the entire document to any 14-point font of your choice.
8. Bold the first occurrence of the words *byte, kilobyte, megabyte, gigabyte,* and *terabyte.*
9. Give the paragraphs a ½ inch first-line indent.
10. Save the document as **Bytes**.
11. Copy the first paragraph and paste it between the second and third paragraphs.
12. Cut the paragraph you just pasted and paste it at the beginning of the document.
13. Delete the paragraph you just pasted and correct any extra or missing blank lines at the beginning of the document or between paragraphs.

When working with computers, you will often see file sizes and memory sizes referred to using terms like byte, kilobyte, megabyte, and gigabyte. Understanding these terms can make working with computers easier.

A byte is roughly enough memory or disk space to store one character of data. A double-spaced page of text requires approximately 1000 bytes of storage. To run Windows 95, Microsoft recommends that you have at least 8 million bytes of random access memory installed in your computer. To install Windows 95 on your hard disk requires approximately 35 to 40 million bytes of disk space.

Because the number of bytes required for many tasks is so large, prefixes from the metric system have been borrowed to describe storage sizes. A thousand bytes is referred to as a kilobyte. For example, a file may require 16 kilobytes of disk space (written as 16K or 16KB). A million bytes is referred to as a megabyte. A hard disk may store 850 megabytes (written as 850M or 850MB). Hard disks now are commonly measured in gigabytes (a billion bytes). For example, you may see a hard disk that stores 1.6 gigabytes (1.6G or 1.6GB).

14. Add the title **Measuring Memory and Storage** to the top of the document. Create one blank line between the title and the first paragraph.
15. Center the title and change the font size to 18 point. Remove the first-line indent from the title.
16. Save the document again.
17. Print the document and exit **WordPad**.

# Challenge Exercise

In reality, a kilobyte is not exactly a thousand bytes, a megabyte is not exactly a million bytes, a gigabyte is not exactly a billion bytes, and a terabyte is not exactly a trillion bytes. This is because, for technical reasons, computers count in a number system based on twos rather than tens. A kilobyte, for example, is actually 1024 bytes, which is 2 raised to the 10th power.

1. Start **WordPad**.

2. In a blank document, key the paragraph shown at left.

3. Save the document in RTF format as **Byte Details**.

4. Create a new document.

5. Open **Byte Details**. (Hint: You will have to specify the RTF format in the Files of Type box in the Open dialog box.)

6. Select the entire document by using the Select All command.

7. Copy the text to the Clipboard.

8. Open the document you created in the Unit 5 Reinforcement Exercise (**Bytes**).

9. Paste the paragraph at the end of the document.

10. Change the font and font size of the new paragraph as necessary.

11. Adjust spacing between paragraphs if necessary and set the first-line indent for the new paragraph.

12. Save the document in Word 6 format as **Byte Complete**.

13. Print the document.

14. Exit **WordPad**.

# LESSON
# 50

**Storage Devices and Organization**

## ►SKILL PRACTICE

### Storage Devices

A computer system typically includes at least two storage devices: a hard drive and a floppy disk drive. Many computer systems include a second floppy disk drive and/or a CD-ROM drive. A key role of the operating system is to allow access to these storage devices. Applications software can access these devices by communicating with the operating system. The operating system must also provide a way for the computer user to access the storage devices of the system. Windows 95 provides access to the storage devices on your computer with the My Computer icon.

Double-clicking the My Computer icon displays a window that shows the storage devices on your computer system, similar to the one shown in Figure 6-1. The contents of each storage device is organized using a system of *folders* and *files*. Because a storage device may contain thousands of files, files are grouped and stored within folders. Folders can include other folders to further subdivide the files within a folder.

> **NOTE**
> A file can contain a document, a program, or data required by the operating system.

> **NOTE**
> Folders are sometimes called directories.

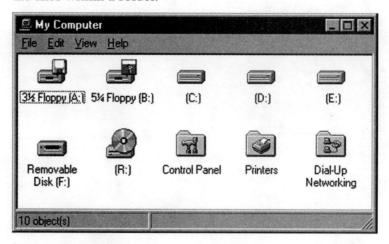

Figure 6-1 My Computer

GLOSSARY TERMS

FILE • a program or document stored on a computer's storage device.

FOLDER • an item used to organize files into groups.

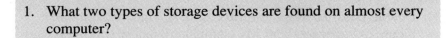

►**ACTIVITY**

1. What two types of storage devices are found on almost every computer?

2. Name a storage device that is optional but is part of many computer systems.

3. What is the role of the operating system in regard to storage devices?

4. What feature of Windows 95 allows you to access the storage devices of your computer?

5. What are used to organize the files on a storage device?

UNIT 6

LESSON

51

Opening Drives and
Folders

In this lesson, you will learn how to
use the My Computer icon to open
drives and folders.

## ►SKILL PRACTICE

**TIP** The drive
letter assigned
to each
storage device is
also displayed in
the My Computer
window under
each icon to
help you identify
the storage
devices.

**NOTE** By default, a
new window
is displayed
each time a
storage
device or folder
is opened. In the
next lesson, you
will learn how to
set an option
that allows you
to browse
through folders
in one window
rather than
opening a new
window with
each folder. If,
during this skill
practice, only
one window is
used to display
the contents of
the folders, the
option has been
changed from
the default.

### Opening Drives

1.  Double-click the **My Computer** icon. A window similar to
    Figure 6-2 appears. Your My Computer window will likely vary
    slightly from the figure.

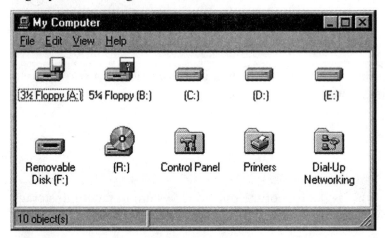

Figure 6-2 The My Computer Window

2.  Double-click the icon that corresponds to your hard drive. If you
    have more than one hard drive icon, click the hard drive from
    which your computer starts (the C: drive).

### Opening Folders

3.  Double-click the **Windows** folder. You may need to scroll the
    contents of the window to find the Windows folder. The
    Windows folder opens.

4.  Close all open windows.

►ACTIVITY

Figure 6-3 Browsing Using the My Computer Icon

1. Open the **My Computer** window.

2. Open the hard disk labeled with the drive letter C.

3. Open the folder named **Program Files**.

4. Open the folder named **Accessories**. Your screen should appear similar to Figure 6-3.

5. Close the **Accessories** window.

6. Close the **Program Files** window.

7. Open the **Windows** folder.

8. Close all open windows.

# LESSON 52

## Browsing Folders Using One Window

In this lesson, you will learn how to browse through folders using one window.

---

## ►SKILL PRACTICE

### To Browse Folders Using One Window

1. Double-click the **My Computer** icon. The My Computer window opens.

2. Pull down the **View** menu from the menu bar that appears near the top of the My Computer window, as shown in Figure 6-4.

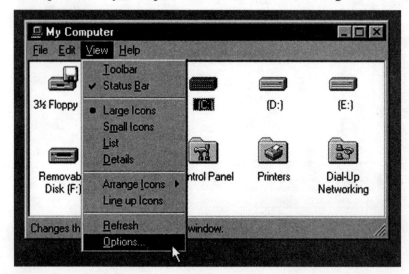

Figure 6-4 The View Menu

3. Choose **Options** from the **View** menu. The Options dialog box appears (see Figure 6-5).

4. If the Folder section is not already displayed, click the **Folder** tab of the Options dialog box.

5. Choose the option labeled **Browse folders using a single window that changes as you open each folder**.

6. Click **OK**.

7. Open the **C:** drive hard disk icon. The current window changes to display the contents of the hard disk.

8. Open the **Windows** folder. Again, the same window displays the requested contents.

*(continued on next page)*

> **TIP** When browsing using one window, refer to the title bar of the window for the name of the current folder.

►ACTIVITY

*Skill Practice* (continued)

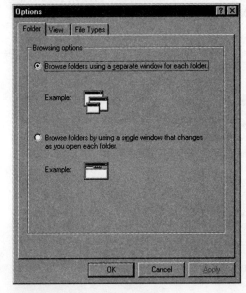

Figure 6-5 Options Dialog Box

## To Browse Using Separate Folders

9. With the Windows folder open, choose **Options** from the **View** menu. The Options dialog box appears.

10. Choose the option labeled **Browse folders using a separate window for each folder**.

11. Click **OK**.

12. Open the **System** folder that is found in the Windows folder. A new window is created to display the contents of the System folder.

13. Close both open windows.

1. Open the **My Computer** window.

2. Open the hard disk labeled with the drive letter C.

3. Open the folder named **Program Files**.

4. Open the folder named **Accessories**.

5. Close all the open windows except the My Computer window.

6. Set the option that causes browsing to occur using a single window.

7. Open the **C:** drive again.

8. Open the folder named **Program Files**.

9. Open the folder named **Accessories**.

10. Close the **Accessories** window and open the **My Computer** window.

11. Set the option that causes browsing to occur using separate windows.

12. Close the **My Computer** window.

# LESSON

# 53

**Navigating with the Toolbar**

In this lesson, you will learn to use the toolbar in folder windows to navigate through folders.

## ▶SKILL PRACTICE

**NOTE**

By default, the toolbar is hidden. If the toolbar is visible before step 2, skip to step 3.

**TIP**

Remember, if you rest the mouse pointer on a toolbar button, the name of the button will appear.

## To Display the Toolbar

1. Open the **My Computer** window.

2. Choose **Toolbar** from the **View** menu. The toolbar appears below the menu bar, as shown in Figure 6-6.

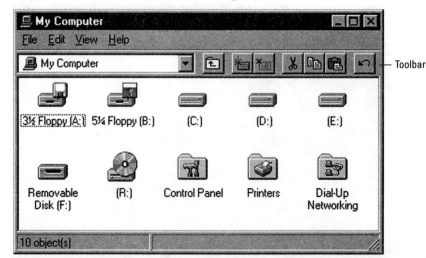

Figure 6-6 The Toolbar

3. If necessary, move and resize the window to display the entire toolbar.

## Using the Toolbar to Back Up One Level

4. Set the option that causes browsing to occur using a single window.

5. Open the **C:** drive window.

6. Open the **Windows** folder.

 7. Click the **Up One Level** button on the toolbar. The contents of the C: drive appear again.

 8. Click the **Up One Level** button again. The My Computer window appears.

*(continued on next page)*

► **ACTIVITY**

1. Open the **My Computer** window.

2. Hide the toolbar if it is visible.

3. Open the **C:** drive.

4. Open the folder named **Program Files**.

5. Open the folder named **Accessories**.

6. Display the toolbar.

7. Use the **Up One Level** button to return to the **Program Files** window.

8. Use the **Go to a Different Folder** box to return to the **My Computer** window.

9. Set the option that causes folders to be browsed using separate windows.

10. Hide the toolbar.

11. Close the window.

*Skill Practice* (continued)

## Using the Go to a Different Folder Box

9. Click the arrow at the end of the **Go to a Different Folder** box, as shown in Figure 6-7. A list of devices and folders appears.

10. Choose **Recycle Bin** from the scrolling list. The window displays the contents of the Recycle Bin.

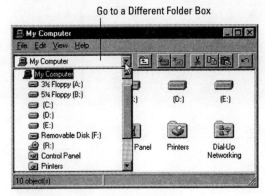

Go to a Different Folder Box

Figure 6-7 Go to a Different Folder Box.

## To Hide the Toolbar

11. Choose **Toolbar** from the **View** menu. The toolbar is hidden.

12. Close the **Recycle Bin** window.

UNIT 6

LESSON

54

View Options

In this lesson, you will learn to use
the My Computer view options.

## ►SKILL PRACTICE

### To View by Small Icon

1. Open the **My Computer** window.

2. Choose **Small Icons** from the **View** menu. The contents are displayed with smaller icons.

### To View by Large Icon

3. Choose **Large Icons** from the **View** menu. The contents are displayed using the standard, large icons.

### To View in List Form

4. Choose **List** from the **View** menu. The contents appear in a list, displaying small icons.

### To View Details

5. Choose **Details** from the **View** menu. The contents appear in a list, displaying additional information about the items in the list (see Figure 6-8).

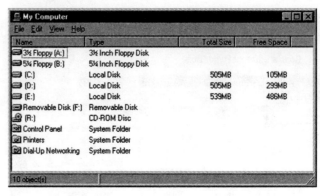

Figure 6-8 Details View

6. Open the **C:** drive window.

7. Open the **Windows** folder and maximize it.

8. If not already in Details view, choose **Details** from the **View** menu. The filename, type, size, and date modified are listed.

*(continued on next page)*

► **ACTIVITY**

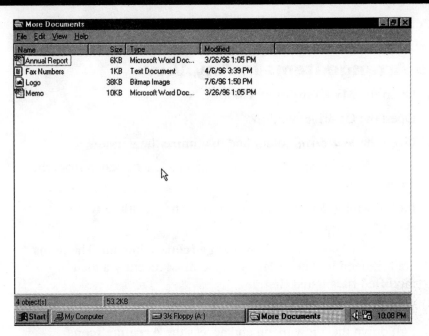

Figure 6-9 Details View

1. Open the **My Computer** window and maximize it.

2. Use the toolbar to switch among all four available views.

3. Switch to **Large Icons** view.

4. Place your work disk in the floppy drive and open the floppy drive's window.

5. Open the **More Documents** folder.

6. Maximize the **More Documents** window.

7. Use the **View** menu to view the documents in **List** view.

8. Use the **View** menu to switch to **Small Icons** view.

9. Switch to **Details** view. Your screen should appear similar to Figure 6-9.

10. Restore the **More Documents** window.

11. Close all windows except the **My Computer** window.

12. Restore the **My Computer** window and close it.

*Skill Practice (continued)*

## To Switch Views Using the Toolbar

9.  Display the toolbar.

10. Click the **Small Icons** button.

11. Click the **List** button.

12. Click the **Details** button.

13. Click the **Large Icons** button.

14. Restore the window by clicking the Restore button on the title bar.

15. Close all windows.

**Arranging and Sorting Items**

In this lesson, you will learn to sort items in folders.

## ►SKILL PRACTICE

In each view, you can arrange the icons or sort the list by name, size, type, and date.

### To Arrange Items in Any View

1.  Open the **My Computer** window.

2.  Open the **C:** drive window.

3.  Open the **Windows** folder and maximize the window.

4.  If not already in large icon view, choose **Large Icons** from the **View** menu.

5.  Pull down the **View** menu and access the **Arrange Icons** submenu.

6.  Choose **by Date** from the **Arrange Icons** submenu. The items are arranged in date order, with the most recently added or modified files listed first.

7.  Switch to small icon view.

8.  Pull down the **View** menu and access the **Arrange Icons** submenu.

9.  Choose **by Size** from the **Arrange Icons** submenu. The items are arranged in file size order, with the smallest files appearing first.

10. Switch to **List** view.

11. Pull down the **View** menu and access the **Arrange Icons** submenu.

12. Choose **by Name** from the **Arrange Icons** submenu. The items are sorted alphabetically by name.

13. Switch to **Details** view.

14. Pull down the **View** menu and access the **Arrange Icons** submenu.

15. Choose **by Type** from the **Arrange Icons** submenu. The items are sorted by type.

*(continued on next page)*

**NOTE** When items are arranged, folders are sorted first, followed by files.

► **ACTIVITY**

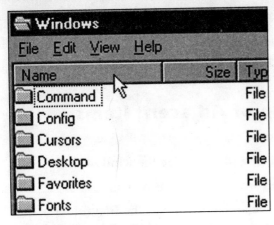

Figure 6-10 Category Headings

1. Open the **My Computer** window.
2. Set the option that causes browsing to occur in a single window.
3. Open the **C:** drive window.
4. Open the **Windows** folder.
5. Open the **System** folder.
6. Maximize the window.
7. View the contents by **Details**.
8. Use the category headings to sort the items by date from oldest to newest.
9. Switch to **Large Icons** view.
10. Arrange the items by Name.
11. Restore the window.
12. Set the option that causes browsing to occur in multiple windows.
13. Close the window.

*Skill Practice (continued)*

## To Sort Items using Category Headings in Details View

16. Click the **Name** category heading, as shown in Figure 6-10. The items are sorted by name, from A to Z.

17. Click the **Name** category heading again. The items are sorted by name, from Z to A.

18. Click the **Size** category heading. The items are sorted from smallest to largest.

19. Switch to **Large Icons** view.

20. Restore the Windows window and close all windows.

**TIP** When you click any of the category headings a second time, the sort order is reversed.

**LESSON 55** *Arranging and Sorting Items*

## LESSON

# 56

**Selecting Items**

In this lesson, you will learn to select items in folders.

## ►SKILL PRACTICE

### To Select an Item

1. Open the **My Computer** window.
2. Click the icon that represents your floppy disk drive **A:**. The item is selected.

### To Select a Group of Adjacent Items

3. Open the **C:** drive window.
4. Open the **Windows** folder and maximize the window.
5. View by large icons and arrange the items by name.
6. Position the pointer above and to the left of the first folder at the top of the window, as shown in Figure 6-11.
7. Begin a selection box by positioning the pointer above and to the left of the area you want to select.
8. Click and drag a selection box around the first two folders in the first two rows (see Figure 6-12). The actual folders selected is not important. All icons in the selection box will be selected.

Figure 6-11 Position the Pointer

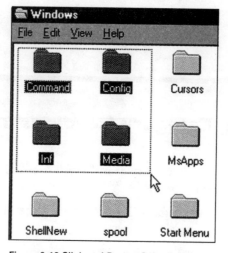

Figure 6-12 Click and Drag a Selection Box

*(continued on next page)*

▶ **ACTIVITY**

Figure 6-13 The Ctrl key allows you to select nonadjacent icons.

*Skill Practice (continued)*

9. Click in a blank area of the window to deselect the items.

10. Drag another selection box. This time, select all the icons in the top three rows.

## To Select Nonadjacent Items

11. Click in a blank area of the window again to deselect the items.

12. Click the **Command** folder to select it.

13. Hold down the **Ctrl** key and click the **Start Menu** folder.

14. Hold down the **Ctrl** key and click the **System** folder.

15. Hold down the **Ctrl** key and click the **Calc** icon.

16. Click a blank area of the window to deselect the items.

17. Restore the **Windows** window.

18. Close all open windows.

1. Open the **My Computer** window.

2. Open the **C:** drive window.

3. Open the **Windows** window and maximize it.

4. Switch the view to small icons and arrange the items by name.

5. Select the **Notepad** icon. You may have to scroll to find the Notepad icon.

6. Select the **Help** folder.

7. Select a group of about ten adjacent icons.

8. Select the entire second column of icons by dragging a selection box beginning at the top of the column. When the selection box reaches the bottom of the window, the contents will scroll until you reach the bottom of the column.

9. Select the following non-adjacent icons: the **System** folder, the **Calc** icon, the **Help** folder, and the **Command** folder (see Figure 6-13).

10. Restore the **Windows** window and close all open windows.

**NOTE**
Dragging a selection box to the edge of a window will cause the window to scroll.

UNIT 6

LESSON

57

**Copying and Moving
Items Among Folders**

In this lesson, you will learn to copy
and move items among folders.

## ►SKILL PRACTICE

## To Copy Items Using Copy and Paste

1. Place your work disk in the floppy disk drive.

2. Open the **My Computer** window.

3. Open the window that shows the contents of your work disk.

4. Open the **Letters** folder and the **Reports** folder and arrange the windows side-by-side.

5. Select the document named **Amy**.

6. Choose **Copy** from the **Edit** menu in the **Letters** folder window.

7. Click in the **Reports** window to make it the active window.

8. Choose **Paste** from the **Edit** menu in the **Reports** window. The Amy document is copied to the Reports window. You may see a dialog box that illustrates the copy process with animated flying paper.

TIP

If the toolbars are displayed, you can use the Copy and Paste buttons to copy files.

## To Move Items Using Cut and Paste

9. Select the document named **Notes for Fall Convention** in the Reports window.

10. Choose **Cut** from the **Edit** menu or click the **Cut** button on the toolbar. The document's icon becomes dimmed to show that it is about to be moved.

11. Click in the **Letters** window to make it the active window.

12. Choose **Paste** from the **Edit** menu or click the **Paste** button on the toolbar. The document is moved to the Letters folder.

## To Move Items by Dragging Their Icons

13. Verify that the **Letters** window and **Reports** window are both visible on the screen.

14. Position the pointer on the **Notes for Fall Convention** document and hold the left mouse button down.

15. Drag the icon from the **Letters** window to the **Reports** window and release the mouse button over the **Reports** window. The document is moved to the Reports folder.

*(continued on next page)*

►ACTIVITY

1.  Use Copy and Paste to copy the document named **Summer Convention** to the **Letters** folder.

2.  Open the **My Computer** window (if it's not already open). Position the window in such a way that makes the My Computer window visible without covering the Letters or Reports windows. You screen should appear similar to Figure 6-14.

3.  While holding down the **Ctrl** key, drag the document named **Kim** to the icon of the floppy drive that contains your work disk. The file is copied.

4.  Open the window that shows the contents of your work disk. Locate the document named Kim that you copied.

5.  Drag the document named **Kim** over the **Letters** folder and release the mouse button when the Letters folder is highlighted. A message will appear, alerting you that a document by the same name already exists in the Letters folder.

6.  Click **Yes** to replace the document with the one you are moving.

7.  Use Cut and Paste to move the **Casper** document from the Reports window to the Letters window.

8.  Click **Yes** when prompted to replace the document in the Letters folder.

9.  Arrange the icons in the **Letters** window by name.

10. Arrange the icons in the **Reports** window by name.

11. Close all open windows.

Figure 6-14 Files can be copied and moved by dragging them between folders.

---

*Skill Practice (continued)*

## To Copy Items by Dragging Icons

16. Select the document named **Casper** in the Letters window.

17. While holding down the **Ctrl** key, drag the document to the **Reports** window.

**TIP** You can also drag an item to another folder using the right mouse button. When you release the mouse button, a menu appears from which you can choose to either move or copy the item.

**TIP** You can duplicate a file within the same folder by highlighting the icon, choosing Copy, and then choosing Paste. A copy of the file will appear in the same folder. The pasted file will have the same name as the original, but the name will begin with the words *Copy of.*

LESSON

# 58

**Copying and Moving
Items to Another Disk**

In this lesson, you will learn to copy
and move items among disks.

## ►SKILL PRACTICE

## To Copy an Item to Another Disk

When a file is dragged to a folder that exists on another disk drive or
to the icon of another disk drive, the file will be copied by default
with no need to hold down the Ctrl key.

1.  Place your work disk in the floppy disk drive if it is not already
    there.

2.  Open the **My Computer** window.

3.  Open the window that shows the contents of your work disk.

4.  Open the **Reports** folder and arrange the windows in such a way
    that the Reports and My Computer windows are both fully
    visible.

5.  Drag the document named **Southwest Expedition** from the
    Reports folder to the **C:** drive icon in the My Computer window.
    The file is copied to the C: drive.

6.  Make the **Reports** window active and display the toolbar if it is
    not already visible. You may have to resize the window to make
    the entire toolbar visible.

 7.  Select the document named **Summer Convention** in the Reports
    folder and click the **Copy** button on the toolbar.

8.  Open the **C:** drive window and paste the document in the C:
    drive window. The document is copied to the C: drive.

## To Move an Item to Another Disk

If you want to move a file to another disk drive by dragging, hold
down the Shift key to override the default and cause the file to be
moved rather than copied.

9.  Locate the **Southwest Expedition** document in the C: drive
    window.

10. Position the windows in such a way that the **C:** drive window
    and the **Reports** window are both visible.

11. Select **the Southwest Expedition** document.

*(continued on next page)*

## ►ACTIVITY

1. Open the **More Documents** folder on your work disk.

2. Copy the document named **Memo** to the **C:** drive.

3. From the **C:** drive window, send the **Memo** document to the work disk in the floppy drive.

4. Using Cut and Paste, move the **Memo** document from the **C:** drive to the **Letters** folder on the floppy disk.

5. Close all open windows.

***Skill Practice*** (*continued*)

12. While holding down the **Shift** key, drag the **Southwest Expedition** document from the **C:** drive window to the **Reports** window. A message will appear, asking if you want to replace the existing file.

13. Click **Yes**. The document moves from the C: drive to the Reports folder on the floppy disk.

## To Send an Item to a Floppy Disk

A shortcut allows you to quickly copy a file to a floppy disk.

14. Make the **C:** drive window active.

15. Select the document named **Summer Convention**.

16. Right-click the document's icon. A shortcut menu appears, as shown in Figure 6-15.

17. From the **Send to** submenu, choose the floppy drive that contains your work disk. The document is copied to the work disk.

18. If it is not already selected, highlight the **Summer Convention** document in the C: drive window.

19. Choose **Cut** from the **Edit** menu.

20. Make the **Reports** window active and choose **Paste** from the **Edit** menu.

21. Click **Yes** when prompted to replace the existing file.

22. Close all open windows.

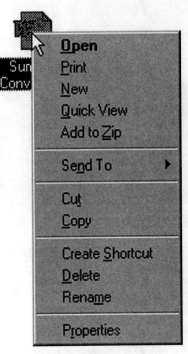

Figure 6-15 The shortcut menu allows you to easily send a file to a floppy disk.

LESSON

## 59

**Renaming Documents and Folders**

In this lesson, you will learn to rename documents and folders.

## ►SKILL PRACTICE

### To Rename a Document or Folder

1. Open the window that shows the contents of your work disk.

2. Open the **More Documents** folder and view the contents by large icon.

3. Click the document named **Fax Numbers** to select it.

4. Pause a second or two and click once more directly on the name of the document. The name will become ready for editing.

5. Key **Fax List** as the new filename and press **Enter**.

6. Close the **More Documents** folder.

7. With the **More Documents** folder selected, click on the name of the folder to prepare it to be edited.

8. Press the **left arrow**. The highlight disappears, and a cursor is visible in the folder name.

9. Press the **left arrow** repeatedly until the cursor is to the left of the word *Documents*. The folder should appear similar to Figure 6-16.

10. Press **Backspace** until the word *More* is deleted.

11. Press **Enter**.

Figure 6-16 You can edit a document or folder name much as you edit other text.

> **NOTE**
>
> Click with care. If you click the second time too quickly, the document may open.

►**ACTIVITY**

1. Open the folder you renamed Documents.
2. Change the name of the **Fax List** document back to **Fax Numbers**.
3. Close the window.
4. Change the name of the **Documents** folder back to **More Documents**.
5. Close all open windows.

LESSON

# 60

**Undoing File and Folder Operations**

In this lesson, you will learn how to undo file and folder operations.

## ►SKILL PRACTICE

### To Undo an Operation

1. Open the window that shows the contents of your work disk.

2. Change the name of the **Reports** folder to your first name and press **Enter**.

3. Choose **Undo Rename** from the **Edit** menu.

   Or

   Click the **Undo** button on the toolbar.

   The original name is restored.

### To Undo a Series of Operations

You can undo a series of file or folder operations by repeatedly choosing Undo.

4. Change the name of the **Reports** folder to your last name.

5. Open the **Letters** folder.

6. Select the document named **Kim** and choose **Copy** from the **Edit** menu.

7. Choose **Paste** from the **Edit** menu to duplicate the document.

8. Select the document named **Amy** and choose **Cut** from the **Edit** menu.

9. Open the **More Documents** folder and choose **Paste** from the **Edit** menu. The document named Amy is moved to the More Documents folder.

10. Choose **Undo Move** from the **Edit** menu. The document named Amy is moved back to the Letters folder.

11. Choose **Undo Copy** from the **Edit** menu. A message appears asking if you want to delete the copy of the file.

12. Click **Yes**.

13. Choose **Undo Rename** from the **Edit** menu. The Reports folder is renamed.

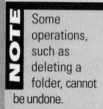

**NOTE** Some operations, such as deleting a folder, cannot be undone.

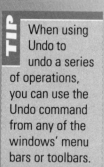

**TIP** When using Undo to undo a series of operations, you can use the Undo command from any of the windows' menu bars or toolbars.

## ►ACTIVITY

1. Change the name of the **Letters** folder to **My Letters**.

2. Copy the document named **Amy** from the **My Letters** folder to the **C:** drive.

3. Move the document named **Casper** from the **My Letters** folder to the **Reports** folder.

4. Change the name of the **Reports** folder to **My Reports**.

5. Undo the four actions taken in the steps above.

6. Close all open windows.

Creating a New Folder

In this lesson, you will learn how to create a new folder.

## ►SKILL PRACTICE

### To Create a New Folder

1. If your work disk is not in the floppy drive, insert it in the drive.
2. Open the work disk window.
3. Pull down the **File** menu.
4. Click **New** and then choose **Folder** from the New submenu. A new folder appears, ready to accept a name.
5. Key **My Folder** as the folder name and press **Enter**.
6. Open the **My Folder** folder.
7. Right-click in the **My Folder** window to access the shortcut menu, as shown in Figure 6-17.
8. Access the **New** submenu and choose **Folder**. A folder appears in the My Folder window.
9. Name the new folder **Nested Folder** and press **Enter**.

> **TIP**
> You can only create a new folder from the File menu when no items in the window are selected.

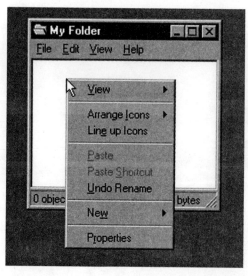

Figure 6-17 You can create a folder from a shortcut menu.

►**ACTIVITY**

Figure 6-18 Folders can be created within folders.

1. Create a new folder named **Another Folder** in the **My Folder** window.

2. Arrange the folders in the **My Folder** window by name. The window should appear similar to Figure 6-18.

3. Close all open windows.

# LESSON

# 62

**Opening and Printing a Document from Its Icon**

In this lesson, you will learn how to open a document by double-clicking its icon and how to print a document from a shortcut menu.

## ►SKILL PRACTICE

## To Open a Document from its Icon

When you double-click a document, Windows loads the program that created the file and automatically loads the document.

1. If your work disk is not in the floppy drive, insert it in the drive.
2. Open the work disk window.
3. Double-click the icon of the document named **Letter of Application**. WordPad starts and loads the document.
4. Exit the program.

## To Print a Document from its Icon

5. Select the document named **Printing from an Icon**.
6. Right-click the document's icon. A shortcut menu appears.
7. Choose **Print** from the shortcut menu. Notepad loads and the document prints. Notepad will automatically exit after sending the document to the printer.

## ►ACTIVITY

1. Open the document named **Printing from an Icon** by double-clicking the icon.

2. Exit **Notepad**.

3. Print the document named **Poster** from its icon.

4. Close all open windows.

In this lesson, you will learn to use Quick View to view the contents of a document.

► **SKILL PRACTICE**

## To View a Document with Quick View

1. If your work disk is not in the floppy drive, insert it in the drive.

2. Open the work disk window.

3. Select the document named **About Quick View**.

4. Right-click the icon. A shortcut menu appears.

5. Choose **Quick View** from the shortcut menu. The contents of the document appear in Quick View.

## To Open the File for Editing

Because Quick View does not allow editing, you must load the program that created the document in order to edit the document.

6. Choose **Open File for Editing** from the **File** menu. Notepad starts and loads the document.

7. Add the following sentence to the document:

   **Quick View cannot open every kind of document.**

8. Save the document.

9. Exit **Notepad**.

10. Close all open windows.

**NOTE** Quick View does not install automatically when Windows 95 is installed. If Quick View does not appear in the shortcut menu when you right-click the Notepad document in step 4, Quick View is not installed on your system.

**NOTE** Quick View cannot open every type of file. If the Quick View option does not appear when you right-click a file icon, no viewer is available for that file type.

LESSON

# 63

## ACTIVITY

1. Use Quick View to view the contents of the document named **Printing from an Icon**.

2. Open the file for editing.

3. Delete the second sentence.

4. Exit **Notepad** without saving.

5. Close all open windows.

# UNIT 6

# Reinforcement Exercise

1. Open the **My Computer** window.
2. Verify that browsing will occur in separate windows.
3. Open the **C:** drive window.
4. Open the **Windows** folder.
5. Open the **System** folder.
6. Open any of the folders visible in the System folder.
7. Close all open windows except for the My Computer window.
8. Set the option that causes browsing to occur in a single window.
9. Open the same series of folders you opened in steps 3 through 6 above.
10. View the toolbar if it is not already visible.
11. Maximize the window.
12. Use the toolbar to switch among all four views.
13. Switch to Details view and sort by name.
14. Switch to Large Icons view and arrange by size.
15. Use the **Up One Level** button as many times as necessary to return to the **My Computer** window.
16. Set the option that causes browsing to occur in separate windows.
17. Open the **Windows** folder and select the **Start Menu** folder.
18. Switch to List view and select the first row of adjacent items.
19. Select the **Command** and **Help** folders.
20. Open the **Letters** folder on your work disk.
21. Use Copy and Paste to copy the document named **Kim** to the **More Documents** folder.
22. In the **More Documents** folder, change the name of **Kim** to **Kim 2**.
23. Move the document named **Kim 2** from the **More Documents** folder to the **Letters** folder.
24. Use Undo to undo the operations you performed in steps 23, 22, and 21.
25. Create a new folder on the work disk. Name the folder **Just for Practice**.
26. Open the **Just for Practice** folder and create a folder inside it named **Empty**.
27. Print the document named **Letter of Application** from its icon.
28. Use **Quick View** (if available) to view the contents of the document named **United Nations**.
29. Exit **Quick View** and close all open windows.

# Challenge Exercise

1. Open the **My Computer** window.

2. View the contents in Details view.

3. On paper, record the names of each storage device in the **My Computer** window.

4. Also, record the type, total size, and free space reported in the window for each device.

5. View the contents by large icon.

6. Open the **Windows** folder on the **C:** drive.

7. View the contents by detail and sort by name in descending order.

8. View the contents by size from largest to smallest.

9. Select two of the smallest nonadjacent files from the **Windows** folder.

10. Use the **Send to** shortcut to send the files to your work disk.

11. View the contents of the **Windows** folder by large icon.

12. Open the work disk window.

13. Move the two files you copied from the **Windows** folder to the **Just for Practice** folder.

14. Close all open windows.

# LESSON 64

### Deleting a File or Folder

In this lesson, you will learn to delete a file or folder. Deleting moves a file or folder into the Recycle Bin, where it stays until the Recycle Bin is emptied.

## ►SKILL PRACTICE

**NOTE** When deleting items from a floppy disk, the items are deleted immediately, rather than waiting in the Recycle Bin.

**NOTE** If a copy of the document named Amy is not in the Reports folder, copy the file from the Letters folder to the Reports folder.

**TIP** You can delete more than one file or folder at a time by selecting the items you wish to delete, right-clicking on one of the items, and choosing Delete.

### To Delete a File or Folder by Dragging

1. If your work disk is not in the floppy drive, insert it in the drive.
2. Open the work disk window.
3. Arrange the windows to make the Recycle Bin icon on the desktop visible.
4. Drag the folder named **Just for Practice** to the Recycle Bin. A message appears, asking if you are sure you want to remove the folder and all its contents.
5. Click **Yes**. The folder is removed from the floppy disk.

### To Delete a File or Folder by Right-Clicking

6. Open the **Reports** folder.
7. Select the document named **Amy**.
8. Right-click the document's icon. A shortcut menu appears.
9. Choose **Delete** from the shortcut menu. You will be prompted to verify your intention to delete.
10. Click **Yes**. The document is deleted.

### To Delete a File or Folder Using the Delete Key

11. On your work disk, select the document named **Memo** that is outside the More Documents folder.
12. Press the **Delete** key. You are prompted to verify your intention to delete.
13. Click **Yes**. The document is deleted.
14. Close all open windows.

# ►ACTIVITY

1. Open the work disk window.

2. Open the **My Folder** folder.

3. Delete the folder named **Another Folder** by dragging it to the Recycle Bin.

4. Close the **My Folder** window.

5. Delete the **My Folder** folder using the shortcut menu.

6. Using the Delete key, delete the document named **Summer Convention** from the work disk window (not from the Reports folder).

7. Arrange the remaining icons in the work disk window.

8. Close all open windows.

# LESSON

# 65

**Restoring Deleted Items and Emptying the Recycle Bin**

In this lesson, you will learn to open the recycle bin, restore a deleted item, and empty the Recycle Bin.

---

## ►SKILL PRACTICE

## To Open the Recycle Bin

1. If your work disk is not in the floppy drive, insert it in the drive.

2. Open the work disk window.

3. Copy the document named **Poster** and the document named **The Internet** to the **C:** drive.

4. Open the **C:** drive window.

5. Delete the document named **Poster** and the document named **The Internet** from the **C:** drive.

6. Close all open windows.

7. Double-click the **Recycle Bin** icon on the desktop. The Recycle Bin window appears.

8. If necessary, change the view to Details view.

9. Maximize the **Recycle Bin** window. Your screen should look similar to Figure 7-1.

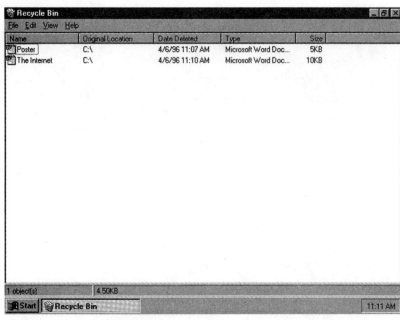

Figure 7-1 The Recycle Bin Window

*(continued on next page)*

# ►ACTIVITY

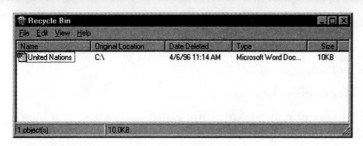

Figure 7-2 Deleted documents appear in the Recycle Bin.

*Skill Practice* (continued)

## To Restore an Item in the Recycle Bin

10. In the **Recycle Bin** window, select the document named **The Internet**.

11. Choose **Restore** from the **File** menu. The document is returned to the **C:** drive.

12. Open the **C:** drive window and locate the document named **The Internet**.

13. Delete the document again to move it back to the **Recycle Bin**.

## To Empty the Recycle Bin

To permanently delete the items in the Recycle Bin, you must empty the Recycle Bin.

14. Make the **Recycle Bin** window active and restore the window.

15. Choose **Empty Recycle Bin** from the **File** menu. A message will appear, asking you to verify your intention to delete the items.

16. Click **Yes**.

17. Close all open windows.

1. Copy the document named **United Nations** from the work disk to the **C:** drive.

2. Drag the **United Nations** document from the **C:** drive to the **Recycle Bin**.

3. Open the **Recycle Bin**. The window should appear similar to Figure 7-2.

4. Restore the document to the **C:** drive.

5. Switch to the **C:** drive window and delete the file using the shortcut menu.

6. Close all open windows.

7. Empty the **Recycle Bin** by right-clicking the Recycle Bin icon and choosing Empty Recycle Bin from the shortcut menu.

**TIP** You can empty the Recycle Bin without opening the Recycle Bin window by right-clicking the Recycle Bin icon and choosing Empty Recycle Bin from the shortcut menu that appears.

**NOTE** Remember, when deleting items from a floppy disk, the items are deleted immediately, rather than waiting in the Recycle Bin.

LESSON

**66**

**Copying a Document to the Desktop**

In this lesson, you will learn how to copy a document to the desktop. It is sometimes useful to have some commonly used documents appear on the desktop for quick access.

## ►SKILL PRACTICE

**NOTE** When an item is copied to the desktop, it is saved in a folder named Desktop in the Windows folder of the drive from which Windows 95 booted.

**NOTE** Because the desktop is actually stored on the C: drive, you must hold down the Ctrl key when dragging an item from the C: drive to the desktop to prevent the file from being moved rather than copied. In some cases, however, you may want to move the item rather than copy it.

### To Copy a Document to the Desktop

1. If your work disk is not in the floppy drive, insert it in the drive.

2. Open the work disk window.

3. Open the **Reports** folder.

4. Drag the document named **Notes for Fall Convention** to a blank area on the desktop.

5. Close all the windows.

6. Drag the document in line with the other desktop objects.

# ►ACTIVITY

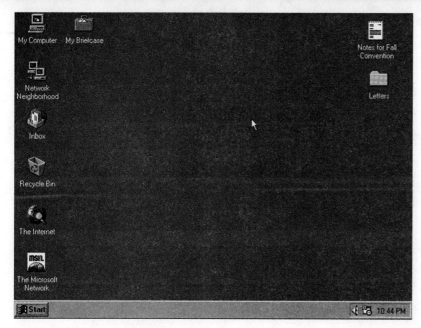

Figure 7-3 Desktop items can be arranged for the most convenience.

1. Copy the **Letters** folder from your work disk to the desktop.

2. Open the **Letters** folder on the desktop.

3. Close all windows.

4. Drag the **Letters** folder and the **Notes for Fall Convention** document to the right edge of the screen, as shown in Figure 7-3.

5. Drag the **Letters** folder to the **Recycle Bin**.

6. Open the **Recycle Bin**.

7. Choose **Select All** from the **Edit** menu.

8. Choose **Restore** from the **File** menu. The Letters folder appears on the desktop.

9. Close the **Recycle Bin**.

10. Delete the **Letters** folder and the **Notes for Fall Convention** document and empty the **Recycle Bin**.

LESSON

# 67

**Saving a Document to the Desktop**

In this lesson, you will learn how to save a document to the desktop.

## ▶SKILL PRACTICE

### To Save a Document on the Desktop

1. Start **WordPad**.

2. Key the following sentence into a blank WordPad document.

   **Documents that are used frequently can be saved to the desktop.**

3. Choose **Save As** from the **File** menu. The Save As dialog box appears.

4. Choose **Desktop** from the **Save in** list box, as shown in Figure 7-4.

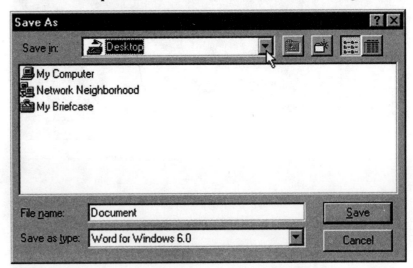

Figure 7-4 You can save on the desktop from the Save As dialog box.

5. Key **Desktop Document** as the filename.

6. Click **Save**.

7. Exit **WordPad**.

8. Locate the icon of the document you just saved on the desktop.

9. Drag the icon to the **Recycle Bin**.

10. Right-click the **Recycle Bin** icon. A shortcut menu appears.

11. Choose **Empty Recycle Bin** from the shortcut menu. A message appears, asking you to verify your intention to delete.

12. Click **Yes**.

# ►ACTIVITY

1. Open the document named **Letter of Application** from your work disk.

2. Replace the address at the top of the document with your return address.

3. Use the **Save As** command to save the document on the desktop.

4. Exit **WordPad**.

5. Leave the document on the desktop for use in an upcoming lesson.

6. Close all open windows.

LESSON

# 68

**The Documents Menu**

In this lesson, you will learn how to use the Documents menu.

## ►SKILL PRACTICE

### To Use the Documents Menu

1. Click the **Start** button. The Start menu appears.

2. Choose **Documents**. The Documents menu appears, showing as many as fifteen of the most recently opened documents.

3. Click outside the menu to close it without choosing a document.

4. If your work disk is not in the floppy drive, insert it in the drive.

5. Open the work disk window.

6. Double-click the document icon named **Printing from an Icon**. The document loads into the Notepad.

7. Exit **Notepad**.

8. Click the **Start** button and display the **Documents** menu. Notice that the **Printing from an Icon** document is listed.

9. Choose **Printing from an Icon**. The document loads into the Notepad.

10. Exit **Notepad**.

**TIP**
Use the Documents Menu to quickly access documents you have recently used.

# ►ACTIVITY

1. Double-click the document named **Poster** on your work disk. The document loads in WordPad.

2. Open the document named **Opening Documents** from your work disk.

3. Exit **WordPad**.

4. Use the **Documents** menu to open the document named **Poster**.

5. Exit **WordPad**.

6. Close all open windows.

LESSON

# 69

**Clearing the Documents Menu**

In this lesson, you will learn how to clear the Documents menu. This is useful when you want to clean up the Documents menu after the documents listed are no longer likely to be opened again.

## ►SKILL PRACTICE

### To Clear the Documents Menu

1. Open the **Start** menu and access the **Documents** menu. Notice that documents are listed.

2. Click outside the menu to close it.

3. Right-click a blank area on the taskbar. A shortcut menu appears.

4. Choose **Properties** from the shortcut menu. The Taskbar Properties dialog box appears.

5. Click the **Start Menu Programs** tab, as shown in Figure 7-5.

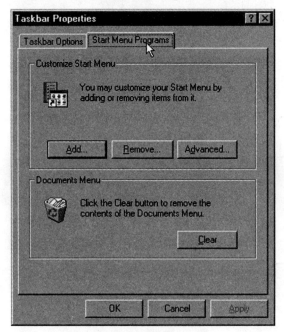

Figure 7-5 Taskbar Properties Dialog Box

6. Click the **Clear** button.

7. Click **OK**.

8. Open the **Start** menu and access the **Documents** menu. The Documents menu is empty.

9. Click outside the menu to close it.

## ►ACTIVITY

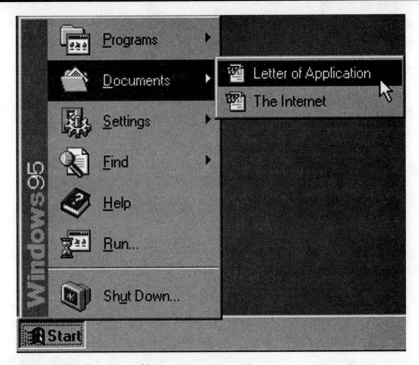

Figure 7-6 The Documents Menu

1. Double-click the document on the desktop named **Letter of Application**. WordPad starts and loads the document. Note: If the document does not appear on the desktop, open it from your work disk.

2. Choose **Open** from the **File** menu. The Open dialog box appears.

3. Open the document named **The Internet** from your work disk.

4. Exit **WordPad**.

5. Open the **Start** menu and access the **Documents** menu. The documents you just opened appear in the Documents menu, as shown in Figure 7-6.

6. Close the menu without choosing a document.

7. Close all open windows.

## ►SKILL PRACTICE

### To Arrange Items on the Desktop

1. If your work disk is not in the floppy drive, insert it in the drive.

2. Copy the **Letters** folder from your work disk to the desktop.

3. Drag some or all of the objects on the desktop to appear across the top of the screen, as shown in Figure 7-7. The objects on your screen may vary from the ones in the figure. Do not attempt to align the icons perfectly.

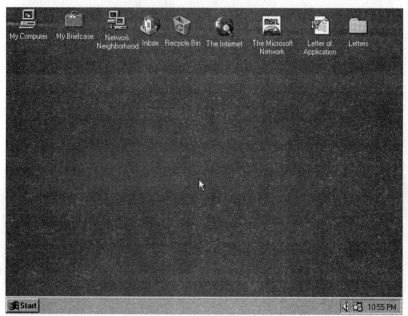

Figure 7-7 Items on the desktop can be moved to any location on the screen.

4. Right-click in a blank area of the desktop. A shortcut menu appears.

5. Choose **Line Up Icons** from the shortcut menu. The objects align.

6. Right-click in a blank area of the desktop. The shortcut menu appears again.

7. Choose **Arrange Icons** and choose **by Name** from the submenu. The objects return to the left edge of the screen.

*(continued on next page)*

## ►ACTIVITY

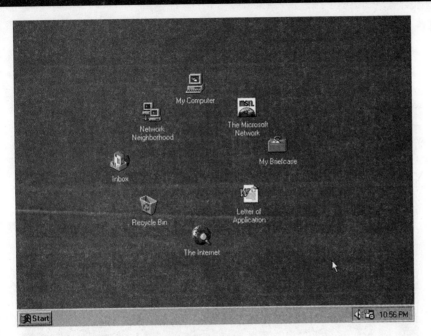

Figure 7-8 A Creative Way to Arrange Desktop Items

1. Arrange some or all of the items on the desktop in a circle, as shown in Figure 7-8.

2. Right-click a blank area of the desktop. A shortcut menu appears.

3. Choose **Line up Icons** from the shortcut menu. The items align into a rectangular shape.

4. Right-click a blank area of the desktop. A shortcut menu appears.

5. Choose to arrange icons by name. The items return to the left edge of the screen.

*Skill Practice (continued)*

## To Auto Arrange Items

The Auto Arrange feature arranges desktop items each time an object is moved, deleted, or added.

8. Right-click the desktop to access the shortcut menu.

9. Choose **Arrange Icons** and choose **Auto Arrange** from the submenu.

10. Drag the **Letters** folder to the center of the screen. As soon as you release the mouse button, the Letters folder is moved back into alignment.

11. Copy the document named **United Nations** from your work disk to the desktop. The icon is automatically aligned. (You may need to move some windows to see this.)

12. Drag the **Letters** folder and the **United Nations** document to the **Recycle Bin**.

13. Empty the **Recycle Bin**.

14. Right-click the desktop to access the shortcut menu.

15. Choose **Arrange Icons** and choose **Auto Arrange** to deselect the feature.

16. Close any windows that may be opened.

# LESSON 71

## Capturing Screens and Windows

In this lesson, you will learn how to capture the contents of the screen or a window for use in a document.

## ►SKILL PRACTICE

### To Capture the Screen

1. Open the **My Computer** window and move it near the center of the screen. Size it to appear similar to Figure 7-9. Close any other open windows.

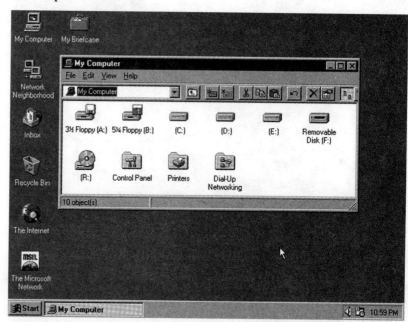

Figure 7-9 The Print Screen key will capture the entire screen image.

2. Press the **Print Screen** key. A graphic of the current screen is copied to the Clipboard.

3. Start **Paint** from the **Accessories** menu.

4. Choose **Paste** from the **Edit** menu. The picture of the screen appears in the Paint document.

5. Choose **Print** from the **File** menu. The Print dialog box appears.

6. Click **OK**. The captured screen prints.

7. **Minimize** Paint.

*(continued on next page)*

> ►ACTIVITY

1. Double-click the **Letter of Application** document on the desktop to open it.
2. Maximize **WordPad**.
3. Capture the screen to the clipboard.
4. Start **Paint**.
5. Paste the captured screen into a Paint document.
6. Print the Paint document.
7. Minimize **Paint**.
8. In WordPad, choose **Paragraph** from the **Format** menu.
9. Capture the window.
10. Click **Cancel** to close the dialog box.
11. Position the cursor at the end of the document and press **Enter**.
12. Choose **Paste** from the **Edit** menu. The image of the Paragraph dialog box appears.
13. Choose **Exit** from the **File** menu. You will be asked if you want to save changes.
14. Click **Yes**. The document saves.
15. Click the **Paint** button on the taskbar.
16. Choose **New** from the **File** menu. Do not save the current document.
17. Choose **Paste** from the **Edit** menu. The image of the Paragraph dialog box appears in the new document.
18. Print the document and exit **Paint** without saving.

*Skill Practice* (*continued*)

## To Capture a Window

8. Make the **My Computer** window active.

9. Press **Alt + Print Screen**. A graphic of the My Computer window is copied to the Clipboard.

10. Click the **Paint** button on the taskbar.

11. Choose **New** from the **File** menu. You will be asked if you want to save the current document.

12. Click **No**.

13. Choose **Paste** from the **Edit** menu. The picture of the My Computer window appears in the Paint document.

14. Choose **Print** from the **File** menu. The Print dialog box appears.

15. Click **OK**. The captured window prints.

16. Exit **Paint** without saving and close the My Computer window.

# LESSON 72

**Creating a Shortcut**

In this lesson, you will learn how to create an icon that provides a shortcut to another object. Shortcuts allow you to quickly open documents and programs that you use regularly.

## ►SKILL PRACTICE

**TIP** Shortcuts can be placed in any folder. They are most useful, however, on the desktop or in the Start menu.

**NOTE** A shortcut is not a copy of the original file or folder. Whether a file is opened from the original icon or the shortcut icon, the same file on the disk is accessed.

**NOTE** Shortcuts do not have to be named using the word *shortcut*. To make shortcuts easy to identify, an arrow in a small box is added to the icon.

### To Create a Shortcut

1. Open the **My Computer** window.
2. Open the **C:** drive and then the **Windows** folder.
3. Select the file named **Calc** (the Calculator accessory).
4. Choose **Create Shortcut** from the **File** menu.

   Or

   Right-click the **Calc** icon and choose **Create Shortcut** from the shortcut menu.

   A file named Shortcut to Calc appears in the Windows folder.
5. Move the **Shortcut to Calc** file to the desktop.
6. Change the name of the shortcut to **Calculator**. (You may need to close or minimize open windows to see the shortcut on the desktop.)
7. Close all open windows.
8. Double-click the **Calculator** shortcut. The Calculator accessory loads.
9. Close the **Calculator**.
10. Arrange the items on the desktop by name.

## ►ACTIVITY

1. Open the **My Computer** window.

2. Right-click the icon that represents the floppy disk drive that contains your work disk. A shortcut menu appears.

3. Choose **Create Shortcut** from the shortcut menu. A message appears saying that Windows cannot create a shortcut in the My Computer window. The message asks if you want the shortcut created on the desktop.

4. Click **Yes**.

5. Close the **My Computer** window.

6. Double-click the shortcut for your floppy drive. The contents of the work disk appear.

7. Close the work disk window.

# LESSON
# 73

**Creating a Printer Shortcut**

In this lesson, you will learn to create a shortcut to your computer's printer. Dragging a document to a printer shortcut will cause the document to print to that printer.

## ►SKILL PRACTICE

### To Create a Printer Shortcut

1.  Open the **My Computer** window.

2.  Open the **Printers** folder. The printer to which your computer prints has an icon in the Printers folder. You may have more than one printer icon in the Printers folder.

3.  Right-click the icon that represents your printer. If you have more that one printer available to you, right-click the one you print to most often. A shortcut menu appears.

4.  Choose **Create Shortcut** from the shortcut menu. Because a printer shortcut cannot appear in the Printers folder, you are asked if you would like to create the shortcut on the desktop.

5.  Click **Yes**. The printer shortcut is created on the desktop.

6.  Close the **Printers** folder and the **My Computer** window.

### To Use the Printer Shortcut to Print a Document

7.  If your work disk is not in the floppy drive, insert it in the drive.

8.  Open the work disk window using the shortcut on the desktop.

9.  Open the **More Documents** folder on the work disk.

10. Drag the document named **Fax Numbers** to the printer shortcut on the desktop. The document prints.

11. Close all open windows.

**NOTE** The process of dragging an item from one location to another to perform an operation is called *drag and drop*.

GLOSSARY TERMS
DRAG AND DROP • dragging an item
from one location to another to perform
an operation.

LESSON

73

►ACTIVITY

Figure 7-10 Printer Shortcut

1. Drag the existing printer shortcut to the **Recycle Bin**.

2. Empty the **Recycle Bin**.

3. Create a new shortcut to your printer and place it on the desktop.

4. Change the name of the printer shortcut to **My Printer** (see Figure 7-10).

5. Drag the document named **Letter of Application** from the desktop to the **My Printer** shortcut. The document prints.

# LESSON 74

**Shortcut Properties**

In this lesson, you will learn how to view the properties of a shortcut. A shortcut's properties provide information about the file or folder to which the shortcut points.

## ►SKILL PRACTICE

### To View the Properties of a Shortcut

1. Right-click the **Calculator** shortcut on the desktop. A shortcut menu appears.

2. Choose **Properties** from the shortcut menu. The Calculator Properties dialog box appears, as shown in Figure 7-11.

> **NOTE**
> Some of the information in your Propeties dialog box, such as target and start in directories, may differ from the figures in this lesson. Dates shown in the figures will also differ from your screen.

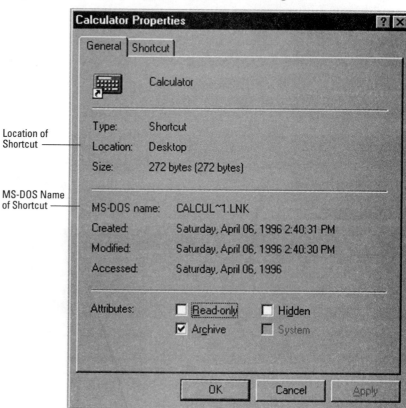

Location of Shortcut

MS-DOS Name of Shortcut

Figure 7-11 General Properties of the Calculator Shortcut

3. Click the **Shortcut** tab in the dialog box. The Shortcut section of the dialog box appears, as shown in Figure 7-12.

*(continued on next page)*

## ►ACTIVITY

1. View the properties of the shortcut to your floppy disk drive.

2. View the properties of the shortcut to your printer. The dialog box should appear similar to Figure 7-13.

3. Close the dialog box.

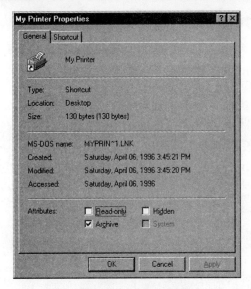

Figure 7-13 Printer Shortcut Properties.

## *Skill Practice* (continued)

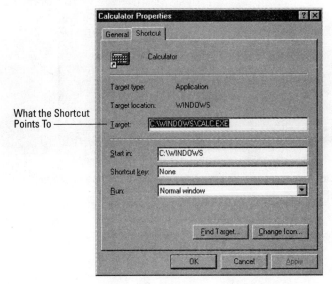

What the Shortcut Points To

Figure 7-12 Shortcut Properties of the Calculator Shortcut.

4. Click **Cancel**.

## LESSON
# 75

**Closing a Minimized Program or Window**

In this lesson, you will learn how to close a minimized program or window.

## ►SKILL PRACTICE

### To Close a Minimized Program or Window

1. Start **WordPad**.

2. Key your name in the document that appears. Do not save.

3. Minimize **WordPad**.

4. Open the **My Computer** window.

5. Minimize the **My Computer** window.

6. Right-click the **My Computer** button on the taskbar. A shortcut menu appears.

7. Choose **Close** from the shortcut menu. The My Computer window closes.

8. Right-click the **WordPad** button on the taskbar. A shortcut menu appears.

9. Choose **Close** from the shortcut menu. You are given an opportunity to save before closing, as shown in Figure 7-14.

10. Click **No**. WordPad exits.

> **TIP**
> Closing a minimized window saves a step because there is no need to restore the window first.

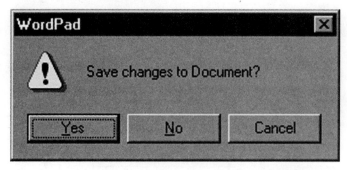

Figure 7-14 Closing a program with unsaved changes generates a message.

► **ACTIVITY**

1. Start the **Calculator** from the desktop shortcut.
2. Minimize the **Calculator**.
3. Close the **Calculator** from the taskbar.

# LESSON 76

In this lesson, you will learn how to customize the taskbar.

## ▶SKILL PRACTICE

### To Move the Taskbar

Move the taskbar to another edge of the screen by dragging it.

1.  Position the mouse pointer over a blank area of the taskbar.
2.  Drag the **taskbar** to the left edge of the screen. The taskbar attaches to the left edge of the screen with the Start button on top.
3.  Drag the **taskbar** to the top of the screen.
4.  Drag the **taskbar** to the right edge of the screen.
5.  Drag the **taskbar** to its original position at the bottom of the screen.

### To Resize the Taskbar

Resize the taskbar by dragging its top edge (innermost edge when moved from bottom of screen).

6.  Position the mouse pointer on the top edge of the **taskbar**. The pointer changes to a double-headed arrow.
7.  Drag the top border of the **taskbar** up about $\frac{1}{2}$ inch. Release the mouse button.

### To Manually Hide the Taskbar

8.  Drag the top border of the **taskbar** to the bottom of the screen and release the mouse button. The taskbar cannot be seen, except for a thin line at the bottom of the screen.
9.  Position the pointer on the line at the bottom of the screen and drag the **taskbar** back to its default size.

*(continued on next page)*

► **ACTIVITY**

*Skill Practice (continued)*

## To Automatically Hide the Taskbar

10. Right-click a blank area of the **taskbar**. A shortcut menu appears.

11. Choose **Properties** from the shortcut menu. The Taskbar Properties dialog box appears, as shown in Figure 7-15.

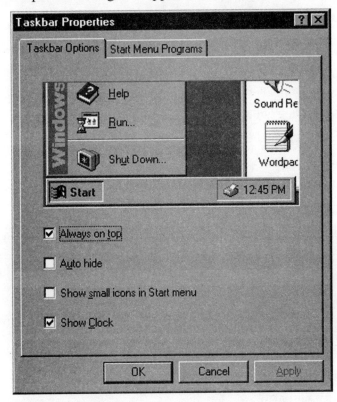

Figure 7-15 Taskbar Properties Dialog Box.

12. Turn on the **Auto Hide** option and click **OK**. The taskbar is hidden.

13. Move the mouse pointer to the bottom of the screen. The taskbar automatically appears.

14. Move the mouse pointer up (away from the taskbar). The taskbar is again hidden.

1. Move the **taskbar** to the right edge of the screen.

2. Select the **My Computer** icon.

3. Move the pointer back to the right edge to make the taskbar appear.

4. Right-click a blank area of the taskbar and choose **Properties** from the shortcut menu.

5. Turn off the **Auto hide** option.

6. Click **OK**.

7. Move the **taskbar** back to the bottom of the screen.

8. Enlarge the **taskbar** to the largest allowable size.

9. Drag the edge of the **taskbar** to the bottom of the screen to hide it.

10. Return the **taskbar** to its default size.

Other taskbar properties include an option to remove the clock from the taskbar and an option to allow windows to overlap the taskbar.

# UNIT 7

# Reinforcement Exercise

1.  Change the name of the **Letter of Application** document on the desktop to **Letter of Application 2**.
2.  If necessary, insert your work disk in the floppy disk drive.
3.  Drag **Letter of Application 2** to the shortcut to your floppy disk drive.
4.  Double-click the shortcut to your floppy disk drive.
5.  Delete the **Letter of Application 2** document from your work disk.
6.  Close the work disk window.
7.  Drag the document named **Letter of Application 2** from the desktop to the **Recycle Bin**.
8.  Restore **Letter of Application 2** to the desktop.
9.  Delete the **Calculator** shortcut.
10. Empty the **Recycle Bin**.
11. Open the document named **Poster** from your work disk.
12. Change the last line of the document to read **60% - 80% OFF**.
13. Save the document to the desktop as **Poster 60-80**.
14. Exit **WordPad**.
15. Load **Poster 60-80** from the **Documents** menu.
16. Exit **WordPad**.
17. Arrange the icons on the desktop by name.
18. Capture the screen, paste it into **Paint**, and print.
19. Minimize **Paint**.
20. Close **Paint** from the taskbar.
21. Print **Poster 60-80** by dragging its icon to the printer shortcut.
22. Drag **Poster 60-80** to the shortcut that points to your work disk.
23. Delete **Poster 60-80** from the desktop.
24. Empty the **Recycle Bin**.

# Challenge Exercise

1. Select the **Letter of Application 2** document, the **My Printer** shortcut, and the shortcut to your floppy disk drive.

2. Drag all three items to the **Recycle Bin**.

3. Empty the **Recycle Bin**.

4. Create a desktop shortcut for each of the storage devices on your computer system. Note: If your system has several, just create shortcuts for three or four of them.

5. Create a desktop shortcut for your printer.

6. View the properties of any one of the storage device shortcuts.

7. Move the **taskbar** to the left edge of the screen.

8. Resize the **taskbar** to about twice the default width.

9. Hide the **taskbar** without using the Auto hide feature.

10. Resize the **taskbar** to approximately the original size.

11. Turn on the **Auto hide** feature.

12. Drag all the desktop items to the right edge of the screen. Note: If your desktop has a large number of desktop items, just drag about five or six of them.

13. Turn off the **Auto hide** feature.

14. Drag the **taskbar** back to the bottom of the screen and return it to the default size.

15. Clear the **Documents** menu.

16. Delete the desktop shortcuts created in this lesson.

17. Empty the **Recycle Bin**.

18. Arrange the icons on the desktop by name.

**Starting the Windows Explorer**

In this lesson, you will learn about the Explorer and how to start it.

## ►SKILL PRACTICE

**NOTE** If you have ever used the File Manager in previous versions of Windows, some features of the Explorer will be familiar to you.

The Explorer is a program that provides an alternative to the My Computer icon. You can use the Explorer to browse a disk, move and copy files, delete files and folders, format and copy disks, and more. You can even run other applications from Explorer.

### To Start the Explorer

1. Click the **Start** button.

2. Choose **Windows Explorer** from the **Programs** menu. The Explorer starts. The Explorer displays two panes (see Figure 8-1). The left pane displays a directory structure of all drives and folders of your computer. The right pane displays the contents of the folder or drive selected in the left pane.

3. Resize the Explorer window, if necessary, to approximate the size of Figure 8-1.

4. Choose **Close** from the **File** menu. The Explorer closes.

**NOTE** The Explorer on your screen may vary from Figure 8-1.

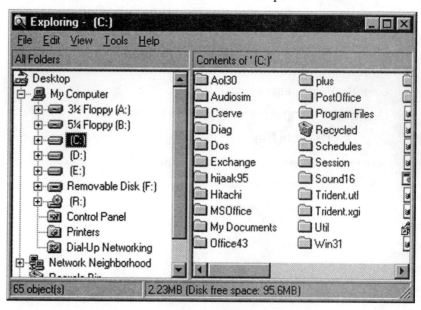

Figure 8-1 The Explorer

*(continued on next page)*

## ►ACTIVITY

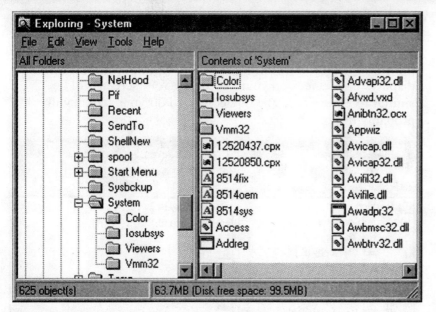

Figure 8-2 The System Folder Displayed in the Explorer

1. Using the **My Computer** window, open the **C:** drive, and then the **Windows** folder.

2. Right-click the **System** folder and start the **Explorer**. The Explorer starts and displays the contents of the System folder. The Explorer appears similar to Figure 8-2.

3. Close the **Explorer**.

4. Close all open windows.

*Skill Practice* (*continued*)

## To Start the Explorer Displaying a Specific Drive or Folder

5. Open the **My Computer** window.

6. If not already in the floppy drive, insert your work disk.

7. Open the window that shows the contents of your work disk.

8. Right-click the **More Documents** folder and choose **Explore** from the shortcut menu that appears. Explorer starts and the right pane displays the contents of the More Documents folder.

9. Close the **Explorer**.

10. Close the window displaying the contents of your work disk.

# LESSON 78

**Expanding and Collapsing Folders**

In this lesson, you will learn how to expand and collapse folders in the Explorer.

## ►SKILL PRACTICE

### To Expand and Collapse Folders

1. Right-click the **My Computer** icon. A shortcut menu appears.

2. Choose **Explore** from the shortcut menu. The Explorer starts and displays the devices on your computer. Your screen will be similar to Figure 8-3. The devices listed on your screen will probably differ.

**NOTE** The hierarchical display in the left pane is sometimes called a *tree*.

**NOTE** You can adjust the amount of space given to each pane by dragging the bar that separates the panes.

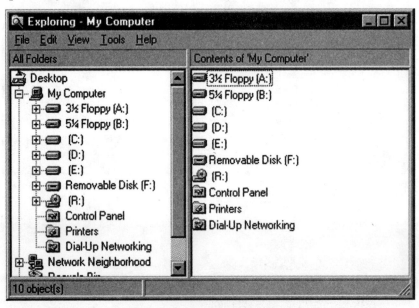

Figure 8-3 The Explorer as Started from the My Computer Icon

Notice in Figure 8-3 that the left pane displays the devices and objects of the desktop. The objects, devices, and folders are displayed in a hierarchical (or outline) form. Also notice that a minus sign (-) appears next to My Computer in the left pane. The minus sign indicates that all the folders (or devices) under that item are visible. Notice that the devices (such as the hard disk drives) have plus signs (+), which indicate that more folders are to be displayed within that folder or device. A plus sign appears only if the folder contains one or more folders. If the folder has only files in it, no plus sign will appear.

*(continued on next page)*

GLOSSARY TERMS

TREE • a hierarchical display of the directory structure of a storage device.

LESSON
78

## ►ACTIVITY

**Skill Practice** (continued)

3. Click the minus sign next to the **My Computer** icon in the left pane. The devices listed under My Computer are no longer listed. The item has been *collapsed*. The box next to the My Computer icon now displays a plus sign to indicate that the item is collapsed (see Figure 8-4).

4. Click the plus sign next to the **My Computer** icon in the left pane. The item is *expanded* to show all the items under it.

5. Click the plus sign next to the icon that represents the **C:** drive. The item is expanded.

6. Click the minus sign that now appears next to the icon that represents the **C:** drive. The item is collapsed.

1. If not already in the floppy disk drive, insert your work disk.

2. In the left pane, click the plus sign next to the icon that represents your work disk.

3. Click on each folder displayed to see the contents of each. The listing will appear in the right pane.

4. Click the minus sign next to the floppy disk drive icon to collapse it.

5. In the left pane, expand the **C:** drive icon.

6. Maximize the **Explorer**.

7. Expand at least three folders on the **C:** drive.

8. Restore and close the **Explorer**.

Figure 8-4 A plus sign indicates a collapsed folder or device.

# LESSON 79

**Browsing a Disk**

In this lesson, you will browse disks and view the contents of folders.

## ►SKILL PRACTICE

### To Browse a Disk

1. Right-click the **My Computer** icon. A shortcut menu appears.
2. Choose **Explore** from the shortcut menu. The Explorer starts and displays the devices on your computer.
3. In the left pane, click the icon that represents the **C:** drive. The contents of the C: drive appear in the right pane.

   The right pane is nearly identical to the windows you see when browsing with the My Computer icon. You can display the same toolbar and choose among the views that you used when browsing with the My Computer icon. When using the Explorer, however, browsing always occurs in a single window. Also, the left pane provides information not available when browsing with the My Computer icon.

### To Display the Toolbar

4. If the toolbar is not already visible, choose **Toolbar** from the **View** menu. The toolbar appears.
5. Double-click the **Windows** folder in the right pane. The contents of the Windows folder appear in the right pane. Also notice that the left pane is updated to show the contents of the C: drive.

### To Start a Program or Open a Document from the Explorer

6. Double-click the **Calc** icon in the **Windows** folder. The Calculator starts.
7. Close the **Calculator**.

### To Quickly Move to Another Device or Folder

The Explorer has the advantage of allowing you to move directly to the contents of any device or folder that you can locate in the left pane.

8. If not already in the floppy disk drive, insert your work disk.
9. In the left pane, click the icon that represents the floppy disk drive that holds your work disk. The contents of your work disk appear in the right pane.
10. Leave the contents of your work disk visible for the Activity that follows.

**TIP** If you cannot immediately locate the Calc icon, sort the contents of the right pane by name.

# ►ACTIVITY

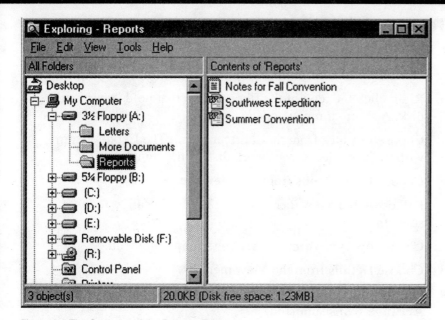

Figure 8-5 The Contents of the Reports Folder

The Explorer should be running, with the contents of your work disk displayed in the right pane.

1.  Double-click the **Letters** folder in the right pane.

2.  Click the **Reports** folder in the left pane. The contents of the Reports folder appear, as shown in Figure 8-5.

3.  Click the **C:** drive icon in the left pane.

4.  Click the **Windows** folder (not the plus sign) in the left pane.

5.  Expand the **Windows** folder in the left pane.

6.  Expand the **System** folder.

7.  Click the **System** folder to display its contents.

8.  Close the **Explorer.**

# LESSON

# 80

**Arranging Icons and Sorting Files**

In this lesson, you will learn to arrange icons and sort files in the Explorer.

## ►SKILL PRACTICE

### To Arrange Icons

1. If not already in the floppy disk drive, insert your work disk.

2. Open the **My Computer** window.

3. Right click the icon of the floppy drive that holds your work disk. A shortcut menu appears.

4. Choose **Explore** from the shortcut menu. The Explorer starts, with the contents of your work disk in the right pane.

5. Choose **Large Icons** from the **View** menu.

6. Pull down the **View** menu and access the **Arrange Icons** submenu.

7. Choose **by Type** from the **Arrange Icons** submenu.

8. Choose **Details** from the **View** menu.

9. Pull down the **View** menu and choose **by Name** from the **Arrange Icons** submenu.

10. Click the icon that represents the **C:** drive in the left pane.

11. Click the plus sign next to the **C:** drive icon in the left pane to expand the device.

12. Click the plus sign next to the **Windows** folder in the left pane to expand the folder.

13. Click the **System** folder to display its contents in the right pane. The contents of the System folder should appear in Details view.

14. Click the **Name** header twice to sort the contents in descending order by name, as shown in Figure 8-6.

15. Close the **Explorer** and all other open windows.

# ►ACTIVITY

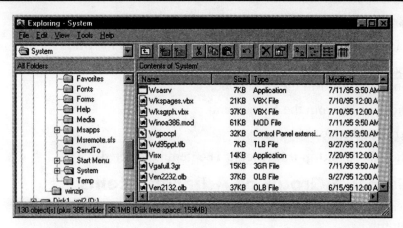

Figure 8-6 You can arrange and sort icons using the same methods you used in the My Computer window.

1. Open the **My Computer** window.

2. Right-click the icon of the floppy drive that holds your work disk and start the **Explorer**.

3. View the contents of the right pane by large icon.

4. Arrange the icons by date.

5. Switch to **Details** view.

6. Using the Name header, sort the contents by name in descending order.

7. Close the **Explorer** and all other open windows.

UNIT 8

LESSON

81

Selecting Objects

In this lesson, you will review the techniques for selecting objects and learn to select all objects and invert a selection.

## ►SKILL PRACTICE

### To Select an Item

1. Start the **Explorer** from the **Programs** menu on the **Start** menu.
2. Locate the **Windows** folder in the left pane and select it. Its contents appear in the right pane.
3. Choose **List** from the **View** menu.
4. Arrange the icons by name.
5. Click the **Desktop** folder icon. The item is selected.

### To Select a Group of Adjacent Items

6. Position the pointer to the left of the first icon in the second column.
7. Drag a selection box around the entire second column of items.

### To Select Nonadjacent Items

8. Click the **Desktop** folder icon.
9. Hold down the **Ctrl** key and click the **System** folder.

### To Invert a Selection

Inverting a selection selects all items that are not currently selected and deselects all selected items. This is useful when you need to select all but a few items. Select the items you do not want selected and then invert the selection.

10. Click the **Calc** icon.
11. Hold down the **Ctrl** key and click the **System** folder. The Calc icon and System folder are selected.
12. Choose **Invert Selection** from the **Edit** menu. All items except the Calc icon and System folder are selected.

### To Select All Items

13. Click the **My Computer** icon in the left pane. The devices of your computer are shown in the right pane.
14. Choose **Select All** from the **Edit** menu. All the items in the right pane are selected.
15. Leave the Explorer open for the Activity that follows.

►ACTIVITY

The Explorer should be running.

1. Display the contents of the **Windows** folder in the right pane.

2. Select the **Start Menu** folder.

3. View by large icon.

4. Select the four folders in the upper left corner of the right pane.

5. Select the **Desktop** folder and the **Help** folder.

6. Invert the selection.

7. Select all items using the **Select All** command. You will be asked if you also want to select hidden files. You will learn about hidden files later in this unit.

8. Click **OK**.

9. Close the **Explorer**.

In this lesson, you will learn to create folders in the Explorer.

## ►SKILL PRACTICE

**TIP** You can also right-click a blank area in the right pane and create a new folder from the shortcut menu that appears.

### To Create a New Folder

1. If not already in the floppy disk drive, insert your work disk.

2. Start the **Explorer** from the **Programs** menu on the **Start** menu.

3. In the left pane, locate the icon of the floppy disk drive that holds your work disk.

4. Click the floppy disk drive icon to display the contents of your work disk in the right pane.

5. Choose **New** from the **File** menu and choose **Folder** from the New submenu.

6. Key **Explorer Folder** as the name for the new folder and press **Enter**.

7. Leave the **Explorer** open for the Activity that follows.

# ►ACTIVITY

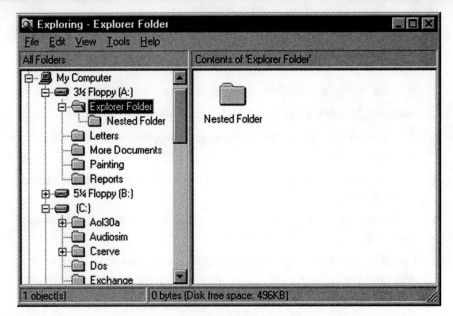

Figure 8-7 The folder named *Explorer Folder* is expanded.

The Explorer should be open, with the contents of your work disk displayed in the right pane.

1. Double-click the folder named **Explorer Folder** in the right pane.

2. Create a folder in **Explorer Folder** named **Nested Folder**.

3. Click the plus sign next to the folder named **Explorer Folder** in the left pane. The new folder appears under the folder named Explorer Folder. Your Explorer should appear similar to Figure 8-7.

4. Close the **Explorer**.

# LESSON 83

## Moving and Copying Files and Folders

In this lesson, you will learn to move and copy files and folders.

## ►SKILL PRACTICE

The Explorer can make moving and copying files easier. You can drag a file or folder from the right pane to the destination in the left pane.

### To Move a File or Folder

1. If not already in the floppy disk drive, insert your work disk.

2. Start the **Explorer** from the **Programs** menu on the **Start** menu.

3. In the left pane, locate the icon of the floppy disk drive that holds your work disk.

4. Click the floppy disk drive icon to display the contents of your work disk in the right pane.

5. In the left pane, expand or collapse folders as necessary to make the **C:** drive icon visible.

6. Using the right mouse button, drag the document named **Letter of Application** to the **C:** drive icon in the left pane. When you release the mouse button, a shortcut menu appears, as shown in Figure 8-8.

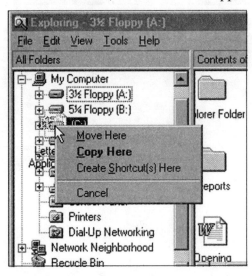

Figure 8-8 Dragging with the right mouse button allows you to choose whether to copy or move the item.

7. Choose **Move Here** from the shortcut menu. The file is moved to the C: drive.

*(continued on next page)*

> **NOTE**
> You can also use Cut, Copy, and Paste to move and copy files in the Explorer.

## ►ACTIVITY

1. Copy the document named **Poster** from the top level of your work disk to the folder named **Explorer Folder**.

2. Open **Explorer Folder**.

3. Move the **Poster** document into the folder named **Nested Folder**.

4. Copy the folder named **Explorer Folder** to the **C:** drive and close the **Explorer**.

*Skill Practice (continued)*

## To Copy a File or Folder

8. Click the **C:** drive icon in the left pane. The contents of the C: drive appear.

9. In the right pane, locate the document named **Letter of Application** that you just copied to the C: drive.

10. Verify that the icon of the floppy disk drive that contains your work disk is visible in the left pane.

11. Using the right mouse button, drag the document named **Letter of Application** from the right pane to the floppy disk drive icon in the left pane. Release the mouse button. A shortcut menu appears.

12. Choose **Copy Here** from the shortcut menu. The file is copied to the floppy disk drive.

13. Display the contents of your work disk.

14. Leave the Explorer open for the Activity that follows.

LESSON

# 84

**Deleting a File or Folder**

In this lesson, you will learn to delete files and folders.

▶**SKILL PRACTICE**

**TIP**
You can also delete a file or folder by right-clicking it in either pane and choosing Delete from the shortcut menu.

**TIP**
You can also empty the Recycle Bin by right-clicking the Recycle Bin in the left pane and choosing Empty Recycle Bin from the shortcut menu.

## To Delete a File or Folder

1. Start **Explorer** and display the contents of the **C:** drive in the right pane.

2. Locate the document named **Letter of Application** in the right pane and select it.

3. Choose **Delete** from the **File** menu. You are asked if you are sure you want to send the document to the Recycle Bin.

4. Click **Yes**. The document is put into the Recycle Bin.

## To Empty the Recycle Bin from the Explorer

5. Click the **Recycle Bin** icon in the left pane. The contents of the Recycle Bin appear in the right pane.

6. Choose **Empty Recycle Bin** from the **File** menu. You are asked to verify your intention to delete.

7. Click **Yes**. The Recycle Bin empties.

8. Leave the Explorer open for the Activity that follows.

## ►ACTIVITY

1. Delete the folder named **Explorer Folder** from your work disk.
2. Delete the folder named **Explorer Folder** from the **C:** drive.
3. Empty the **Recycle Bin** from the Explorer.
4. Close the **Explorer**.

# LESSON
# 85

**Formatting a Floppy Disk**

In this lesson, you will learn to format a disk from the Explorer.

## ►SKILL PRACTICE

For this lesson, you will need an unformatted diskette or a diskette that can be reformatted without losing any important data. Do not use your work disk for this lesson.

### To Format a Floppy Disk

1. Start **Explorer**.

2. Insert a diskette to be formatted into the floppy disk drive.

3. In the left pane, click the **My Computer** icon.

4. In the right pane, click the icon of the floppy drive that contains the disk to be formatted.

5. Choose **Format** from the **File** menu. The Format dialog box appears, as shown in Figure 8-9.

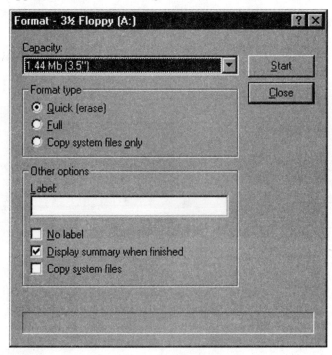

Figure 8-9 Format Dialog Box

**NOTE** The Quick format type simply removes files from a disk that is already formatted. The Full format type reformats the disk and checks for bad spots on the disk. The Copy system files only format type creates a startup disk from an already formatted disk.

*(continued on next page)*

---

►ACTIVITY

Use the Explorer to reformat the floppy disk you formatted in the Skill Practice. Label the disk with your first name.

---

*Skill Practice* (*continued*)

6. Choose the appropriate capacity from the **Capacity** list box. If you are unsure of the capacity, ask your instructor.

7. Select **Full** from the **Format type** options.

8. Click in the **Label** text box and key **New Disk** as the disk label.

9. Click **Start**. Formatting begins. The process of formatting a disk may take a minute or more. When the format is complete, the results of the format are displayed.

10. Click **Close**. The Format dialog box is active.

11. Click **Close**. The Format dialog box closes.

12. Close **Explorer**.

UNIT 8

LESSON

**86**

Copying a Floppy Disk

In this lesson, you will learn to copy a disk from the Explorer.

## ►SKILL PRACTICE

For this lesson, you will need your work disk and the disk you formatted in the previous lesson.

### To Write-Protect a Disk

Before copying a disk, it is a good idea to write-protect the disk you are copying to prevent the original disk from being overwritten accidentally.

1.  If your work disk is in the floppy disk drive, eject it.

2.  Slide the small tab in the corner of the disk to expose the hole. The disk is now write-protected.

### To Copy a Floppy Disk

3.  Start **Explorer**.

4.  Insert your work disk into the floppy disk drive.

5.  In the left pane, click the **My Computer** icon.

6.  In the right pane, click the icon of the floppy drive that contains your work disk.

7.  Choose **Copy Disk** from the **File** menu. The Copy Disk dialog box appears, as shown in Figure 8-10. Your Copy Disk dialog box may vary from the one in the figure.

**NOTE**

If your work disk is a 5 1/4-inch disk, write-protect it by placing a write-protect tab over the notch in the disk.

**TIP**

You can also access the Copy Disk dialog box by right-clicking the floppy drive icon in either pane and choosing Copy Disk from the shortcut menu.

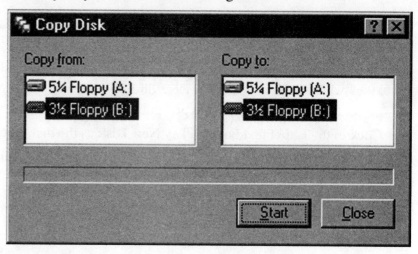

Figure 8-10 Copy Disk Dialog Box

*(continued on next page)*

► ACTIVITY

1. Use the Explorer to copy your work disk again. You may use the same destination floppy disk or another one.

2. Remove the write-protection from your work disk.

3. Close the **Explorer**.

**Skill Practice** (*continued*)

8. In both the **Copy from** and **Copy to** boxes, select the drive that holds your work disk. The selection may already be made for you.

9. Click **Start**. The source disk is read. After the disk has been read, you will be prompted to insert the disk you are copying to.

10. When prompted, eject your work disk and insert the disk you formatted in the previous lesson.

11. Click **OK**. The data are written to the destination disk. When the copy is complete, a message will appear in the Copy Disk dialog box, as shown in Figure 8-11.

12. Click **Close**.

13. Leave the Explorer open for the Activity that follows.

TIP You can copy another disk by clicking Start again or return to the Explorer by clicking Close.

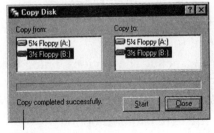

Message area

Figure 8-11 The copy is complete.

# LESSON 87

**Viewing MS-DOS Filename Extensions and Paths**

In this lesson, you will learn to view MS-DOS filename extensions and paths in the Explorer.

## ►SKILL PRACTICE

### To View Extensions

On your disks, files are stored using names that are compatible with MS-DOS. MS-DOS filenames include a three-character filename extension that is used to identify the various types of files. Windows 95 also uses these extensions but usually hides them from your view. You can choose to have the extensions displayed.

1.  Start **Explorer**.
2.  Choose **Options** from the **View** menu. The Options dialog box appears.
3.  If necessary, click the **View** tab. The option called **Hide MS-DOS file extensions...** is selected by default.
4.  Click the **Hide MS-DOS file extensions...** option to deselect it.
5.  Click **OK**. The dialog box closes.
6.  View the contents of the **Windows** folder on the **C:** drive.
7.  View the contents by small icon. Notice that the filenames include extensions. For example, **Calc** is now **Calc.exe**.

### To View the Full MS-DOS Path

In MS-DOS, the *path* is the drive letter and the directories that lead you to a particular file. By default, only the current folder is displayed in the title bar of the Explorer and in the right pane. You can, however, have the full MS-DOS path displayed.

8.  Choose **Options** from the **View** menu. The Options dialog box appears.
9.  Select the **Display the full MS-DOS path in title bar** option.
10. Click **OK**. Notice that the MS-DOS path name appears in the title bar and above the right pane.
11. Double-click the **System** folder in the right pane. The path is extended to include the System folder.
12. Choose **Options** from the **View** menu. The Options dialog box appears.
13. Turn off the **Display the full MS-DOS path in title bar** option.
14. Turn on the **Hide MS-DOS file extensions...** option.
15. Click **OK**.
16. Close the **Explorer**.

**TIP**

Setting the option that displays filename extensions also causes extensions to be displayed when using the My Computer icon to browse a disk. You can also set the filename extension option by choosing Options from the View menu in the My Computer window.

**GLOSSARY** TERMS

PATH • the drive letter and directories that lead to a particular file.

## ►ACTIVITY

1.  Start the **Explorer**.

2.  Set the option that causes filename extensions to be viewed.

3.  Set the option that causes full MS-DOS paths to be viewed.

4.  Close the **Explorer**.

5.  Double-click the **My Computer** icon.

6.  Open the **C:** drive window.

7.  Open the **Windows** folder. Notice the path in the title bar and the filename extensions in the window.

8.  Choose **Options** from the **View** menu.

9.  Click the **View** tab.

10. Deselect the option to display the path.

11. Select the option that hides extensions.

12. Click **OK**.

13. Close all windows.

LESSON

# 88

**Viewing Hidden Files and Folders**

In this lesson, you will learn to view hidden files and folders.

## ►SKILL PRACTICE

### To View Hidden Files and Folders

Disks contain files that are not automatically visible. These files are usually files used by the operating system, but other files and folders may also be hidden.

1. Start **Explorer**.

2. View the contents of the **Windows** folder. Notice that the bottom left corner of the Explorer window tells you how many objects are displayed and how many are hidden.

3. Choose **Options** from the **View** menu. The Options dialog box appears.

4. If necessary, click the **View** tab to display the View section of the dialog box. Notice that the top portion of the dialog box includes a list of file types that the Explorer hides from view (see Figure 8-12).

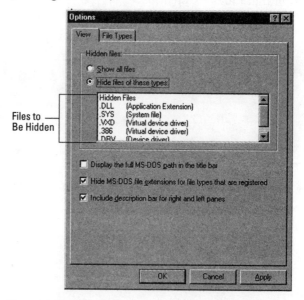

Figure 8-12 Certain types of files are hidden by default.

5. Select the **Show all files** option and click **OK**. *Hidden files and folders* are now visible.

*(continued on next page)*

GLOSSARY TERMS

HIDDEN FILES AND FOLDERS • files and folders that are usually hidden from view.

LESSON

# 88

## ►ACTIVITY

1. Start the **Explorer**.

2. Display the contents of the **Windows** folder.

3. Open the **System** folder.

4. Open the **Iosubsys** folder. Notice how many items are visible.

5. Set the option that makes all files visible. Notice how many items are now visible.

6. Set the option that hides files that are usually hidden.

7. Close the **Explorer**.

*Skill Practice* (*continued*)

6. Choose **Options** from the **View** menu. The Options dialog box appears.

7. Select the **Hide files of these types** option and click **OK**.

8. Close the **Explorer**.

# UNIT 8

# Reinforcement Exercise

1. Start the **Explorer** and display the contents of your work disk.

2. Display the contents of the **C:** drive.

3. Expand the **Windows** folder and all folders within the Windows folder.

4. Collapse all folders and devices.

5. Use the Explorer to locate the accessory named **Calc** in the **Windows** folder and start it from the icon.

6. Close the **Calculator**.

7. View the contents of the **Windows** folder by small icon.

8. Arrange the icons by type.

9. Using the **Invert Selection** command, select all items in the **Windows** folder except the **Help** folder.

10. Create a folder on your work disk named **Temporary Folder**.

11. Copy the **Letters** folder into the folder named **Temporary Folder**.

12. Move the folder named **Temporary Folder** to the **C:** drive.

13. Delete **Temporary Folder** from the C: drive.

14. Empty the **Recycle Bin**.

15. Close the **Explorer**.

# Challenge Exercise

To complete this exercise, you will need two blank or erasable disks in addition to your work disk.

1. Start the **Explorer**.

2. Set the option that allows filename extensions to be viewed.

3. Set the option that allows the full MS-DOS path to be displayed.

4. Set the option that allows hidden files and folders to be viewed.

5. In the left pane, expand the **Program Files** folder on the **C:** drive.

6. Expand every folder within the **Program Files** folder.

7. Locate **WordPad** in the **Accessories** folder in the **Program Files** folder.

8. Start **WordPad** from the Explorer.

9. Exit **WordPad**.

10. Create a folder named **Challenge Folder** on the **C:** drive.

11. Copy the **Reports** folder from your work disk to the **Challenge Folder** on the **C:** drive.

12. Eject your work disk and insert a blank disk or a disk that can be reformatted without losing important data.

13. Format the disk.

14. Move the **Challenge Folder** to the floppy disk you just formatted.

15. Copy the disk that is now in the floppy disk drive to a blank disk or to a disk that can be reformatted without losing important data.

16. Set the option that hides hidden files and folders.

17. Set the option that hides MS-DOS filename extensions.

18. Set the option that prevents the MS-DOS path from appearing.

19. Close the **Explorer**.

# LESSON 89

**Starting Find**

In this lesson, you will learn to start Find from the Start menu, the Explorer, and My Computer.

►**SKILL PRACTICE**

You can right-click the My Computer icon, any device in the My Computer window, or any folder to start Find. Find will then search within that device or folder.

Find allows you to quickly locate a file or folder. You can search by name and location, date modified, size, or type. You can even search for files that contain specified text.

## To Start Find from the Start Menu

1. Click the **Start** button.

2. Choose **Find** from the **Start** menu. The Find menu appears.

3. Choose **Files or Folders** from the **Find** menu. The Find dialog box appears, as shown in Figure 9-1.

4. Choose **Close** from the **File** menu. Find closes.

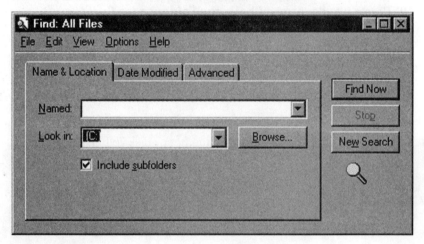

Figure 9-1 Find Dialog Box

## To Start Find from the Explorer

5. Start the **Explorer**.

6. Choose **Find** from the **Tools** menu. The Find menu appears.

7. Choose **Files or Folders** from the **Find** menu. The Find dialog box appears.

8. Choose **Close** from the **File** menu. Find closes.

9. Close the **Explorer**.

*(continued on next page)*

# ►ACTIVITY

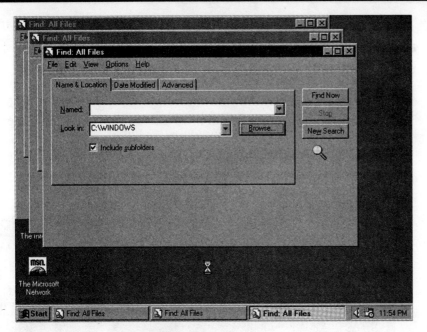

Figure 9-2 You can run Find multiple times.

**Skill Practice** (*continued*)

## To Start Find from the My Computer Window

10. Open the **My Computer** window.

11. Click the **C:** drive icon.

12. Choose **Find** from the **File** menu. The Find dialog box appears.

13. Click the Close button on the Find dialog box. Find closes.

14. Close the **My Computer** window.

## To Start Find by Right-Clicking

15. Right-click the **My Computer** icon. A shortcut menu appears.

16. Choose **Find** from the shortcut menu. The Find dialog box appears.

17. Close **Find**.

1. Start **Find** from the Start menu.

2. Start the **Explorer** while leaving **Find** open.

3. Start **Find** again from the **Explorer**. Two Find windows are now open.

4. Click the **Exploring** button on the taskbar.

5. Close the **Explorer** but leave the Find windows open.

6. Minimize both **Find** windows.

7. Open the **My Computer** window.

8. Open the **C:** drive window.

9. Right-click the **Windows** folder and choose **Find** from the shortcut menu. Notice that the Find dialog box that appears is set to search in the Windows folder.

10. Close the **C:** drive window and the **My Computer** window.

11. Redisplay the minimized **Find** windows. Note: In the Challenge Exercise at the end of this Unit, you will run two searches at the same time by opening two Find dialog boxes.

12. Right-click a blank area on the taskbar and choose to **Cascade** the windows. Your screen should appear similar to Figure 9-2.

13. Close all **Find** dialog boxes.

# LESSON 90

**Finding Files and Folders by Name and Location**

In this lesson, you will learn to find files and folders by name and location.

## ►SKILL PRACTICE

### To Find a File or Folder by Name and Location

1. Click the **Start** button.

2. Choose **Find** from the **Start** menu. The Find menu appears.

3. Choose **Files or Folders** from the **Find** menu. The Find dialog box appears. If necessary, click the **Name & Location** tab to make that section active.

4. If not already in the floppy disk drive, insert your work disk.

5. If necessary, click the **Named** text box.

6. Key **Logo**.

7. Click the arrow in the **Look in** text box and choose the floppy disk drive that holds your work disk, as shown in Figure 9-3.

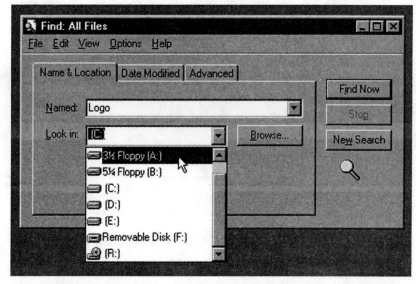

Figure 9-3 The Look in box allows you to narrow the search.

8. Click **Find Now**. A file is found and is displayed in the bottom of the dialog box.

*(continued on next page)*

**TIP** Clicking the Browse button allows you to specify a folder in which to search.

## ►ACTIVITY

1. Use **Find** to locate the document named **Southwest Expedition** on your work disk.

2. Open the folder that contains the document.

3. Close the open window.

4. Close **Find**.

*Skill Practice* (*continued*)

## To Open the Folder That Contains the Located File

9. If necessary, select the **Logo** file at the bottom of the dialog box.

10. Choose **Open Containing Folder** from the **File** menu. The More Documents folder opens.

11. Close the **More Documents** folder.

12. Close **Close** from the **File** menu. Find closes.

# LESSON 91

**Finding Files and Folders by Date Modified**

In this lesson, you will learn to find files and folders by date modified.

## ►SKILL PRACTICE

### To Find a File or Folder by Date Modified

1. Start **Explorer**.
2. Choose **Find** from the **Tools** menu. The Find menu appears.
3. Choose **Files or Folders** from the **Find** menu. The Find dialog box appears.
4. Choose **My Computer** from the **Look in** list.
5. Click the **Date Modified** tab. The dialog box appears as shown in Figure 9-4.

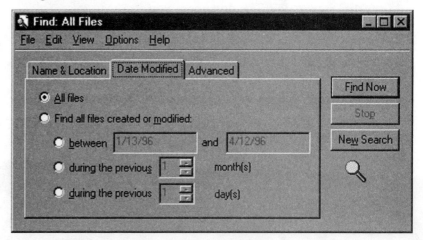

Figure 9-4 Date Modified Section of the Find Dialog Box

6. Click the **Find all files created or modified** option.
7. Click the **during the previous 1 days** option. Leave the number of days set to 1.
8. Click **Find Now**. Find begins searching all storage devices for files created or modified within the last day. The files appear in a list at the bottom of the dialog box. Many of the files listed will be temporary files or operating system files.
9. Close **Find**.
10. Close the **Explorer**.

**NOTE**
Choosing My Computer from the Look in list causes all devices to be searched.

**TIP**
You can click the Stop button to stop a search at any time.

## ►ACTIVITY

1. Start **WordPad**.

2. In the blank document that appears, key **My name is** and key your full name.

3. Save the document on your work disk as **Name Document** and exit **WordPad**.

4. Right-click the **My Computer** icon and choose **Find** from the shortcut menu.

5. Look in **My Computer** for files created or modified during the previous 1 day. The document you just saved in WordPad should appear in the list at the bottom of the dialog box.

6. When you see **Name Document** appear in the list, click **Stop** to stop the search.

7. Click the **New Search** button. A message appears, warning you that your current search will be cleared.

8. Click **OK**.

9. Click the **Name & Location** tab.

10. Choose your work disk from the **Look in** box.

11. Click the **Date Modified** tab.

12. Specify that you want to search for files created or modified during the previous 2 months. (Hint: Click the up arrow in the months box to increment the number of months to 2. The files on your work disk that were created or modified in the last 2 months appear in the list at the bottom of the dialog box.)

13. Click **Find Now**.

14. Close **Find**.

In this lesson, you will learn to find files using two advanced find features. You will search for files by type and by size.

## ►SKILL PRACTICE

### To Find a File by Type

1. Open the **My Computer** window.

2. Right-click the icon of the floppy disk that contains your work disk.

3. Start **Find** from the shortcut menu.

4. Click the **Advanced** tab.

5. Click the arrow in the **Of type** box. An extensive list of every file type registered with your system appears.

6. Choose **Text Document** from the list.

7. Click **Find Now**. Find searches your work disk for text documents. The text documents appear in the list at the bottom of the dialog box.

8. After the search is complete, click **New Search** and click **OK**.

### To Find a File by Size

9. Click the **Name & Location** tab.

10. Choose your work disk from the **Look in** box.

11. Click the **Advanced** tab.

12. Choose **At most** from the **Size is** box.

13. Click in the **KB** box and key **6** (see Figure 9-5).

14. Click **Find Now**. The files that are 6 kilobytes or less in size are listed.

15. Close **Find** and the **My Computer** window.

<table>
<tr><td>
Choosing New Search in step 8 resets the search location. As a result, it is necessary to choose your work disk again in step 10.
</td></tr>
</table>

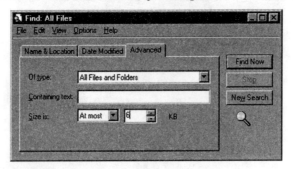

Figure 9-5 Files can be searched by size.

► **ACTIVITY**

1. Start **Find**.

2. Search all the devices on your system for bitmap images.

3. Search all the devices on your system for files of at least 1 megabyte (1000 KB).

4. Search your **C:** drive for files of at least 500KB.

5. Close **Find**.

LESSON

# 93

**Finding Files by the Text Contained in the Files**

In this lesson, you will learn how to find files by searching the text within the files.

## ►SKILL PRACTICE

### To Find a File by the Text it Contains

1.  If necessary, open the **My Computer** window.

2.  Right-click the icon of the floppy disk that contains your work disk.

3.  Start **Find** from the shortcut menu.

4.  Click the **Advanced** tab.

5.  Key **China** in the **Containing text** box.

6.  Click **Find Now**. Find begins searching your work disk for documents that contain the word *China*. One document is found, as shown in Figure 9-6.

7.  Close **Find**.

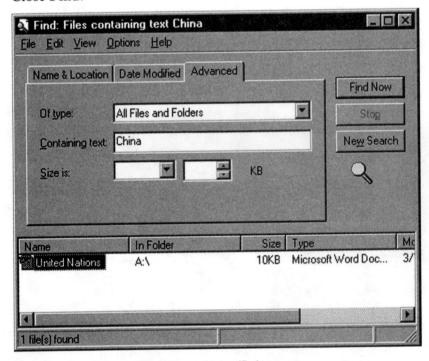

Figure 9-6 Find can locate files that contain specified text.

►**ACTIVITY**

1. Start **Find**.

2. Search your work disk for the document that contains your name. (The document you created in the previous lesson.)

3. Double-click **Name Document** in the list to open the document. You do not have to wait for the entire disk to be searched before opening the document.

4. Exit **WordPad**.

5. Close **Find**.

6. Close the **My Computer** window.

UNIT 9
LESSON
94
Saving Search Criteria and Results

In this lesson, you will learn to save search criteria and search results.

## ►SKILL PRACTICE

### To Save Search Criteria

1. Open the **My Computer** window.

2. Right-click the icon of the floppy disk that contains your work disk.

3. Start **Find** from the shortcut menu.

4. Click the **Advanced** tab.

5. Key **government** in the **Containing text** box.

6. Click **Find Now**. Find begins searching your work disk for documents that contain the word *government*. Two documents are found.

7. Pull down the **Options** menu. The Save Results option should not have a check mark by it. If the option is selected, choose it from the menu to turn off the option.

8. Choose **Save Search** from the **File** menu. The search criteria are saved to the desktop.

9. Close **Find** and the **My Computer** window.

10. The search icon appears on the desktop, as shown in Figure 9-7.

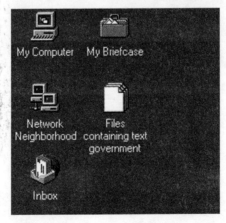

Figure 9-7 Searches are saved to the desktop.

*(continued on next page)*

► **ACTIVITY**

1. Use **Find** to search for any documents on the **C:** drive larger than 300 kilobytes.

2. Save the search criteria without the results.

3. Close **Find**.

4. On the desktop, change the name of the Search icon you just saved to **More than 300K**.

5. Double-click **More than 300K** to start Find with the search criteria.

6. Perform the search.

7. Save the search criteria with the results.

8. Close **Find**.

9. Double-click the Search icon you just saved to start Find and display the results of the last search.

10. Turn off the option that causes results to be saved.

11. Close **Find**.

12. Drag all Search icons to the **Recycle Bin** and empty the Recycle Bin.

---

*Skill Practice (continued)*

## To Use a Saved Search

11. Double-click the Search icon on the desktop. Find starts, and the criteria for the saved search are set.

12. Click the **Advanced** tab to see that the search criteria are set.

13. Click **Find Now**. The search begins. The two files that meet the criteria are found again.

## To Save Search Results

You can save the search results along with the criteria. The list of files found by the search will appear when you double-click the Search icon.

14. Choose **Save Results** from the **Options** menu. The Save Results option is turned on.

15. Choose **Save Search** from the **File** menu.

16. Close **Find**.

17. Another Search icon appears on the desktop. The new Search icon has the same name as the first but has a (2) added to the end of the name.

18. Double-click the new Search icon. Find starts and displays the results of the saved search.

19. Choose **Save Results** from the **Options** menu. The Save Results option is turned off.

20. Close **Find**.

**NOTE** When you save the results with a search, the results that appear when you reload the previous search will not reflect any changes to your computer since the results were saved. You must perform the search again to have an up-to-date list.

# Reinforcement Exercise

1. Start **Find** by right-clicking the **Windows** folder on the **C:** drive.

2. Find the files in the **Windows** folder that were created or modified in the previous month.

3. Start a new search.

4. Key **pad** in the **Named** box and click **Find Now**. Find locates all files with *pad* in the name.

5. Scroll through the list of files found and locate the file named **WordPad** with a file type of Application.

6. Double-click the file to start **WordPad**.

7. Key the following sentence into **WordPad**:

   **Find is a useful and flexible feature of Windows 95.**

8. Save the document on your work disk as **About Find**.

9. Exit **WordPad**.

10. Close **Find**.

11. Start **Find** from the **Start** menu.

12. Search your work disk for documents that contain the text **Windows 95**.

13. Search the **Program Files** folder on the **C:** drive for files that are at least 100 kilobytes in size.

14. Search the same folder for files of type **Application** that are at least 100 kilobytes in size.

15. Save the search criteria but not the results.

16. Close **Find**.

17. Use the search icon on the desktop to repeat the last search.

18. Close **Find**.

19. Delete the Search icon on the desktop.

20. Empty the **Recycle Bin**.

# Challenge Exercise

1. Use **Find** to search for documents on your work disk that contain the text **print**.

2. Save the search and the results.

3. Close **Find**.

4. On your work disk, copy the document named **Printing from an Icon** to the **More Documents** folder.

5. From the desktop, open the saved search. The results of the previous search are visible in the dialog box.

6. Perform the search again. The copy of the file is found in the **More Documents** folder.

7. Close **Find**.

8. Delete the Search icon and empty the **Recycle Bin**.

9. Start **Find** from the **Explorer**.

10. Start **Find** again from the **Start** menu.

11. Close all windows (including the **Explorer**) except for the Find dialog boxes.

12. Tile the **Find** dialog boxes horizontally.

13. Make the top dialog box active.

14. Prepare a search of all devices for files created or modified in the last 3 days. Do not begin the search.

15. Switch to the bottom **Find** dialog box.

16. Begin a search of the **C:** drive for files that are at least 50 kilobytes in size. As soon as the search begins, switch to the top Find dialog box and start the search. Both Find dialog boxes will search simultaneously.

17. Allow both searches to end and close both windows.

# LESSON 95

**Introducing Paint**

In this lesson, you will learn how to start Paint and open and close an existing painting. You will also learn about the Paint window and its parts.

## ►SKILL PRACTICE

Paint is a program that allows you to create pictures, designs, or other graphics. Images you create in Paint can be used in other applications.

### To Start Paint

1. Click the **Start** button.

2. Open the **Programs** menu and then the **Accessories** menu.

3. Click **Paint** in the Accessories menu. Paint starts, as shown in Figure 10-1.

4. If necessary, maximize the **Paint** window.

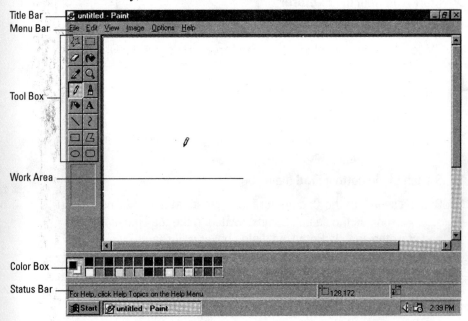

Figure 10-1 The Paint Window

5. Familiarize yourself with the parts of the Paint screen as identified in Figure 10-1.

*(continued on next page)*

# ►ACTIVITY

1. Briefly describe the steps required to start Paint.

2. What is the purpose of the work area in the Paint window?

3. What appears in the tool box?

4. What part of the screen allows you to choose colors while painting?

5. Where does the name of your painting appear?

**Skill Practice** (*continued*)

The Paint window includes the parts you have worked with in other applications: a title bar, a menu bar, and a status bar. The name of your painting appears in the title bar. Paint also includes a work area where you will do your painting. Special parts of the window include the tool box, which is where the <u>drawing tools</u> are located; and the <u>color box,</u> which is a palette of colors from which to choose while painting.

6. Exit **Paint**.

LESSON

# 96

Opening a Drawing

In this lesson, you will learn how to open a drawing.

## ►SKILL PRACTICE

## To Open a Drawing

1. Start **Paint**.

2. Insert your work disk in the floppy disk drive.

3. Choose **Open** from the **File** menu. The Open dialog box appears.

4. Choose the floppy disk drive that contains your work disk from the **Look in** box.

5. Double-click the **Painting** folder on the work disk.

6. Click on the painting named **River**.

7. Click the **Open** button. The River drawing opens.

8. Leave **Paint** open for the Activity that follows.

►*ACTIVITY*

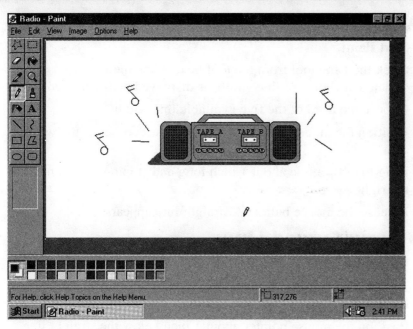

Figure 10-2 An Open Painting

1. Open the document named **Radio** from the **Painting** folder on your work disk. The River painting closes, and a graphic of a radio appears, as shown in Figure 10-2.

2. Open the **River** painting again.

3. Exit **Paint**.

# LESSON 97

**Drawing Lines**

In this lesson, you will learn how to draw straight and curved lines.

---

## ►SKILL PRACTICE

### To Draw Straight Lines

1. Start **Paint**.

2. Click the **Line** tool from the tool box. When the Line tool is selected, a choice of line widths is displayed below the tool box.

3. Choose the third of the five available line widths.

4. Position the mouse pointer near the top left corner of the work area.

5. Drag to draw a line about 1 inch long and sloping down and to the right.

6. Release the mouse button. A straight line appears.

### To Draw Curved Lines

7. Click the **Curve** tool in the tool box. The line width options appear at the bottom of the tool box.

8. Choose the fourth of the five available line widths.

9. Position the mouse pointer about 1 inch below the straight line you drew in the steps above.

10. Drag a line down the screen about 2 inches and release the mouse button. A straight line appears.

11. Position the pointer on the right side of the line, as shown in Figure 10-3.

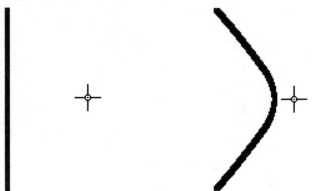

Figure 10-3 Preparing to Curve the Line    Figure 10-4 Drag to adjust the curve.

*(continued on next page)*

► **ACTIVITY**

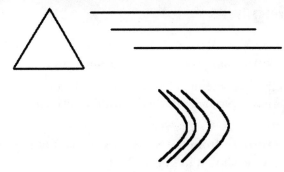

Figure 10-5 These lines were drawn with the Line and Curve tools.

1. Choose **New** from the **File** menu. Do not save changes to the current painting.

2. Practice using the **Curve** tool. Create lines that curve twice.

3. Choose **New** from the **File** menu. There is no need to save.

4. Using the **Line** tool and the **Curve** tool, attempt to duplicate the painting shown in Figure 10-5. (Hint: Use the Shift key when painting to draw the horizontal lines.)

5. Exit **Paint** without saving.

*Skill Practice (continued)*

12. Click and hold down the left mouse button. The line curves toward the pointer.

13. Continue holding down the mouse button and drag to adjust the curve.

14. When your curve looks similar to Figure 10-4, release the mouse button.

15. Without moving the pointer, click again to deactivate the tool.

16. Leave **Paint** open for the Activity that follows.

**TIP**
You can curve a line in two directions. After making your first click to adjust the curve in one direction, click the mouse again to curve the line toward a second point. If you curve a line in two directions, the final click in step 15 is not necessary.

LESSON

98

**Saving and Printing a Painting**

In this lesson, you will learn how to save and print your paintings.

## ►SKILL PRACTICE

### To Save a Painting

1. Start **Paint**.

2. Use the **Line** tool to draw a frame for playing tick-tack-toe.

3. Choose **Save As** from the **File** menu. The Save dialog box appears. If necessary, choose your work disk from the **Save in** box.

4. Choose **Monochrome Bitmap** from the **Save as Type** box at the bottom of the dialog box, as shown in Figure 10-6.

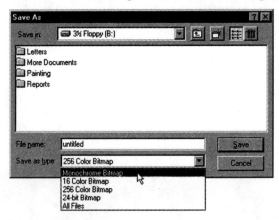

Figure 10-6 The Save Dialog Box

5. If necessary, double-click the **Painting** folder to open it.

6. Key **Tick-Tack-Toe** in the File name box.

7. Click **Save**.

### To Print a Painting

Printing a painting is no different from printing any other document.

8. Choose **Print** from the **File** menu.

9. Click **OK**. The document prints.

►**ACTIVITY**

Figure 10-7 A Star Created with the Line Tool

1. Choose **New** from the **File** menu.

2. Use the **Line** tool to draw a star. (See Figure 10-7.)

3. Save the painting in the **Painting** folder on your work disk as a **monochrome bitmap** and name it **Star**.

4. Print the painting.

5. Exit **Paint**.

**Drawing Shapes**

In this lesson, you will learn how to draw shapes.

## ►SKILL PRACTICE

### To Draw a Rectangle

1. Start **Paint**.

2. Click the **Rectangle** tool.

3. Position the mouse pointer near the top left corner of the work area.

4. Drag down and to the right to draw a rectangle approximately 2 inches tall and 3 inches wide.

5. Release the button.

### To Draw an Ellipse

6. Click the **Ellipse** tool.

7. Position the pointer below the rectangle.

8. Drag an ellipse about the size of an egg.

9. Release the button.

### To Draw a Rounded Rectangle

10. Click the **Rounded Rectangle** tool.

11. Position the mouse pointer in a blank portion of the work area.

12. While holding down the **Shift** key, drag a rounded square about 1 inch in width.

13. Release the button.

14. Save the painting in the **Painting** folder on your work disk as a **monochrome bitmap** named **Shapes**.

15. Print the painting.

16. Leave **Paint** open for the Activity which follows.

# ►ACTIVITY

1. Choose **New** from the **File** menu.
2. Draw a face using only the **Ellipse** tool.
3. Draw a rectangle around the face.
4. Print the painting.
5. Exit **Paint** without saving.

**Using Colors**

In this lesson, you will learn how to use the color box when drawing.

## ▶SKILL PRACTICE

**TIP**

If your screen does not show the Color Box, choose Color Box from the View menu.

**NOTE**

There are three Rectangle Fill options. The first option is the default rectangle with no fill color. The second option creates a rectangle with a border and a fill color. The third option creates a rectangle with a fill color but no border. These same fill options are available for ellipses and rounded rectangles.

Figure 10-9 Rectangle Fill Options

The Color Box allows you to choose a foreground and background color. The foreground color is used for lines and borders of shapes. The background color is used to fill shapes.

### To Choose Colors

To choose the foreground or outline color, left-click the desired color in the Color Box. The foreground color appears in the top color choice box (see Figure 10-8). To choose the background or fill color, right-click on the desired color. The background color appears in the bottom color choice box.

Figure 10-8 The Color Box

1.  Start **Paint**.
2.  With the left mouse button, click a **red** color in the Color Box. The foreground color is set to red.
3.  With the right mouse button, click a **blue** color in the Color Box. The background color is set to blue.

### To Paint with the Selected Colors

4.  Select the **Line** tool.
5.  Choose the widest line width.
6.  Draw a line anywhere in the work area. A red line is drawn.
7.  Select the **Rectangle** tool. Three Rectangle Fill options appear under the toolbox, as shown in Figure 10-9.
8.  Choose the filled rectangle with border from the Rectangle Fill options.
9.  Draw a rectangle anywhere in the work area. The rectangle has a red border and is filled with blue.

*(continued on next page)*

►**ACTIVITY**

1. Start **Paint**.

2. Draw a yellow circle with a black border.

3. Draw a green square with no border.

4. Draw a blue-bordered rounded rectangle with no fill.

5. Select a blue foreground and a red background.

6. Connect the yellow circle and the green square with a blue line.

7. Connect the green square and the blue rectangle with a red line.

8. Exit **Paint** without saving.

*Skill Practice* (*continued*)

## To Paint with the Colors Reversed

You can drag with the right mouse button to reverse the colors.

10. Using the right mouse button, drag another rectangle in the work area. The border and fill colors are reversed.

11. Select the **Line** tool.

12. Using the right mouse button, drag another line in the work area. The line appears in the blue background color.

13. Exit **Paint** without saving.

**Using the Fill With Color Tool**

In this lesson, you will learn how to fill an enclosed area with a color using the Fill With Color tool.

---

## ►SKILL PRACTICE

### To Fill with a Color

1. Start **Paint**.

2. Draw a rectangle with no fill. Make the rectangle about 2 inches tall by 3 inches wide.

 3. Click the **Fill With Color** tool.

4. Using the left mouse button, click a color of your choice from the Color Box.

5. Position the pointer inside the rectangle and click. The rectangle is filled with the selected color.

6. Use the **Line** tool to draw a triangle. Make sure the corners of the triangle are connected.

7. Click the **Fill With Color** tool.

8. Using the left mouse button, click a color of your choice from the Color Box.

9. Position the pointer inside the triangle and click. The rectangle is filled with the selected color.

10. Leave Paint open for the Activity that follows.

## ►ACTIVITY

1. Open the painting named **Star** from the **Painting** folder on your work disk. There is no need to save the current painting.

2. Fill each white area in the star with black.

3. Fill the area outside the star with one of the light patterns in the Color Box.

4. Save the painting as **Star 2**.

5. Print the painting.

6. Exit **Paint**.

UNIT
10

LESSON
102

Erasing and Using Undo

In this lesson, you will learn how to erase and undo in paint.

## ►SKILL PRACTICE

### To Erase

1. Start **Paint**.

2. Select the **Line** tool.

3. Draw a line anywhere in the work area.

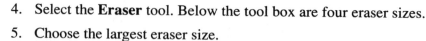

4. Select the **Eraser** tool. Below the tool box are four eraser sizes.

5. Choose the largest eraser size.

6. Drag the eraser over the line until it is completely erased.

### To Undo

You can undo the three most previous operations.

7. Draw a rectangle anywhere in the work area.

8. Draw an ellipse anywhere in the work area.

9. Draw a rounded rectangle anywhere in the work area.

10. Draw a line anywhere in the work area.

11. Choose **Undo** from the **Edit** menu.

12. The line is erased.

13. Choose **Undo** from the **Edit** menu.

14. The rounded rectangle is erased.

15. Choose **Undo** from the **Edit** menu.

16. The ellipse is erased.

17. Pull down the **Edit** menu. Notice that Undo is no longer available.

18. Leave Paint open for the Activity which follows.

## ►ACTIVITY

1. Choose **New** from the **File** menu. Do not save.

2. Draw a circle.

3. Erase the circle completely. If possible, erase the entire circle by dragging the eraser only once or twice.

4. Undo the erase.

5. Exit **Paint**.

UNIT 10

LESSON

103

Using the Selection Tools

In this lesson, you will learn how to use the selection tools. These tools allow you to select rectangular areas or irregularly shaped areas.

## ►SKILL PRACTICE

### To Select an Irregularly Shaped Area

1. Start **Paint**.

2. Draw a rectangle with no fill color about 2 inches tall and 3 inches wide.

3. Below the rectangle, draw a circle with no fill color about 1 inch in diameter.

4. Use the **Fill With Color** tool to fill the rectangle with a dark blue or black and the circle with yellow.

 5. Select the **Free-Form Select** tool.

6. Drag the pointer all the way around the circle, as shown in Figure 10-10. When you release the mouse button, a rectangular frame appears around the circle.

7. Position the pointer over the circle and drag it up to the rectangle. Place the circle in front of the rectangle. Notice how only the circle was selected.

8. Release the mouse button, leaving the circle in front of the rectangle.

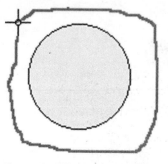

Figure 10-10 The Free-Form Select tool selects irregularly shaped areas.

*(continued on next page)*

## ►ACTIVITY

*Skill Practice (continued)*

## To Select a Rectangular Area

9.   Select the **Select** tool.

10. Drag a rectangle around the circle, as shown in Figure 10-11. Release the mouse button.

11. Position the pointer over the selected rectangle and drag it down about an inch. All of the painting in the rectangle moves with the selection rectangle.

12. Leave Paint open for the Activity which follows.

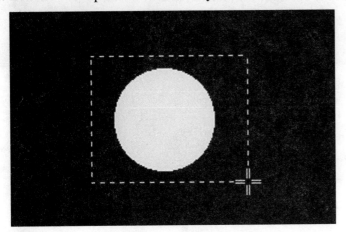

Figure 10-11 The Select tool selects rectangular areas.

1.   Open the painting named **Star** from the **Painting** folder on your work disk.

2.   In an area near the star, draw a rounded rectangle larger than the star with no fill.

3.   Use the **Fill With Color** tool to fill the area with a light pattern from the color box.

4.   Use the **Free-Form Select** tool to select the star.

5.   Move the selected star over the rounded rectangle.

6.   Use the **Select** tool to select the rounded rectangle and the star which appears over it.

7.   Center the selected image in the work area.

8.   Save the painting as **Star 3**.

9.   Print the painting.

10. Exit **Paint**.

# LESSON 104

**Adding Text**

In this lesson, you will learn how to add text to your paintings.

## ▶SKILL PRACTICE

**TIP**

You can edit the text in the text box, change font, style, and size, and resize the text box until the text box is no longer selected. At that point, the text becomes part of the painting and cannot be edited. The only way changes can be made after that point is to erase the text and use the Text tool again.

### To Add Text to a Painting

1. Start **Paint**.

2. From the Color Box, choose a foreground color that appeals to you.

3. Click the **Text** button.

4. Drag a text box in the work area about $\frac{1}{2}$ inch tall and 4 inches wide. A box appears in the work area.

5. Key your name in the text box.

6. If the text toolbar, shown in Figure 10-12, does not appear, choose **Text Toolbar** from the **View** menu.

Figure 10-12 Text Toolbar

7. From the Text toolbar, choose a font that appeals to you.

8. Choose the largest font size that allows your name to fit within the bounds of the box.

9. Leave Paint open for the Activity that follows.

## ►ACTIVITY

1. Choose **New** from the **File** menu. Do not save changes to the current painting.
2. Draw a large red rectangle in the work area.
3. Add the text *Windows 95* over the red rectangle in a dark color or black. Make the text large and bold but keep it within the bounds of the red rectangle.
4. Print the painting.
5. Exit **Paint** without saving.

LESSON

# 105

**Using Paintings in Other Applications**

In this lesson, you will learn how to use paintings in other applications.

## ►SKILL PRACTICE

### To Copy a Painting

1. Open the painting named **Radio** from the **Painting** folder on your work disk.

2. Use the **Select** tool to select the radio and the sounds that surround it.

3. Choose **Copy** from the **Edit** menu.

### To Paste the Painting into Another Application

4. Start **WordPad**.

5. Choose **Paste** from the **Edit** menu. The painting appears in the document, as shown in Figure 10-13.

6. Exit **WordPad** without saving.

7. Leave Paint open for the Activity that follows.

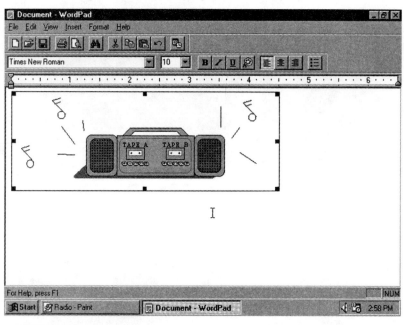

Figure 10-13 Paintings can be copied to other applications.

► **ACTIVITY**

Figure 10-14 This logo can be copied to WordPad or another application.

1. Choose **New** from the **File** menu. Do not save changes.

2. Create a logo similar to the one in Figure 10-14.

3. Select and copy the logo.

4. Start **WordPad**.

5. Press **Enter** several times to create at least four blank lines.

6. Place the cursor at the top of the document.

7. Paste the logo.

8. Click the **Center** button to center the logo on the line.

9. Save the document on your work disk as **Logo Header**.

10. Print the document.

11. Exit **WordPad**.

12. Exit **Paint**.

# UNIT 10

# Reinforcement Exercise

1. Start **Paint**.
2. Open the painting named **Star 2** from the **Painting** folder on your work disk.
3. Create a new painting.
4. Use the **Line** tool and **Ellipse** tool to draw a stick figure.
5. Use the **Curve** tool to draw a small mound for the stick figure to stand on.
6. Save the painting as a **16 color bitmap**. Name the painting **Stick Person**.
7. Draw a square about 1 inch across below the mound.
8. Draw a rounded rectangle next to the stick figure. Make the shape as tall as the stick figure.
9. Fill the rounded rectangle with a color of your choice.
10. Use the **Eraser** tool to erase the square.
11. Use **Undo** to bring back the square.
12. Use the **Eraser** tool to erase the square again.
13. Use the **Text** tool to add your name to the painting.
14. Save the painting again.
15. Print the painting.
16. Exit **Paint**.

1.  Use **Paint** to design a letterhead. Use the **Text** tool to put your name, address, and telephone number on the letterhead. Use any graphics you want to use in the design.

2.  Copy the letterhead to a **WordPad** document.

3.  Save the **WordPad** document as **My Letterhead**.

4.  Print the document.

5.  Close **WordPad** and **Paint**.

LESSON
# 106

**Using the Calculator**

In this lesson, you will learn to use the Calculator.

## ►SKILL PRACTICE

## To Use the Calculator

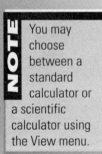

**TIP** You may have to press the Num Lock key to allow numbers to be entered from the keypad.

**NOTE** You can also enter numbers and choose keys on the calculator by clicking the buttons with the mouse.

**NOTE** You may choose between a standard calculator or a scientific calculator using the View menu.

1.  Start the **Calculator** from the **Accessories** menu. The Calculator appears, as shown in Figure 11-1.

2.  Using the numeric keypad, key **725**.

3.  Press the + key on the numeric key pad.

4.  Now key **423**.

5.  Press **Enter**. The answer is displayed.

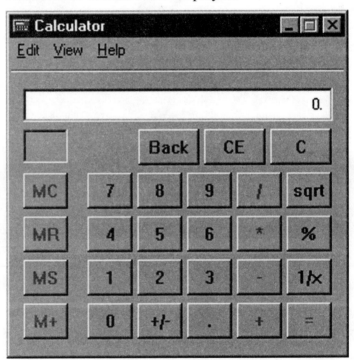

Figure 11-1 The Calculator

*(continued on next page)*

▶ACTIVITY

1. Start the **Calculator**.
2. Use the **Calculator** to solve the following problems:

   **693 + 354 =**

   **5629 * 437 =**

   **6108 / 16 + 1.25 =**

   **56309 * 6 =**

   **4195835 / 3145727 * 3145727 – 4195835 =**
3. Close the **Calculator**.

---

*Skill Practice* (continued)

The table below presents a summary of the functions of the standard calculator.

| Keyboard Function | Equivalent | Description |
|---|---|---|
| MS | Ctrl+M | Save current value in memory |
| MR | Ctrl+R | Recall value from memory |
| M+ | Ctrl+P | Add current value to the value in memory |
| MC | Ctrl+L | Clear memory |
| sqrt | @ | Calculates the square root of the current value |
| % | % | Displays the result of multiplication as a percentage |
| 1/X | R | Calculates the reciprocal of the current value |
| BACK | Backspace | Clear the last keystroke when entering values |
| CE | Delete | Clear the last entry |
| C | Esc | Clear all |

Table 11-1

6. Close the **Calculator**.

# LESSON 107

**Using the Calendar**

In this lesson, you will learn to use the Calendar.

## ►SKILL PRACTICE

**NOTE**

The Calendar is available only if Windows 95 was installed over Windows 3.1. If the Calendar does not appear in your Accessories menu, the program is probably not installed on your computer.

### To Start the Calendar

1. Start **Calendar** from the **Accessories** menu. If Calendar is not in your Accessories menu, see the note in the margin.

### To Open a Calendar

2. Choose **Open** from the **File** menu.

3. Open **sampcal.cal** from your work disk.

### To Move to a Specific Date

4. Choose **Date** from the **Show** menu.
   Or
   Press **F4**.
   The Show Date dialog box appears.

5. Enter **1/3/97** and press **Enter**. The Calendar displays a schedule for the given date.

### To Enter an Appointment

6. Click **1:00**. The cursor is positioned next to 1:00.

7. Key **Meeting with accountant**.

### To Create an Appointment at a Special Time

8. Choose **Special Time** from the **Options** menu. The Special Time dialog box appears.

9. Enter **3:45** in the **Special Time** box and click the **PM** option.

10. Click **Insert**. The special time appears on the schedule.

11. Enter **Racquetball** on the 3:45 line.

### To Save and Exit the Calendar

12. Choose **Save** from the **File** menu.

13. Choose **Exit** from the **File** menu. Calendar closes.

## ►ACTIVITY

1. Start the **Calendar**.

2. Enter your schedule for tomorrow on the appropriate page of the Calendar.

3. Save the calendar on your work disk as **MyCal.cal** and exit **Calendar**.

# LESSON 108

**Using the Cardfile**

In this lesson, you will learn to use the Cardfile.

## ►SKILL PRACTICE

**NOTE**

The Cardfile is available only if Windows 95 was installed over Windows 3.1. If the Cardfile does not appear in your Accessories menu, the program is probably not installed on your computer.

**TIP**

The Cardfile can be used for more than names and addresses. Each card consists of a header and free-form text within the card. The information on each card does not have to follow a specific or consistent format.

### To Start the Cardfile

1. Start **Cardfile** from the **Accessories** menu. If Cardfile is not in your Accessories menu, see the note in the margin.

### To Open a Cardfile

2. Choose **Open** from the **File** menu.

3. Open **sampcrd.crd** from your work disk.

### To Search for a Specific Card

4. Choose **Find** from the **Search** menu. The Find dialog box appears.

5. Enter **Acme** in the **Find What:** box and click **Find Next**. The card that includes the company name Acme Marketing appears.

6. Click **Cancel** to close the Find box.

### To Add a Card

7. Choose **Add** from the **Card** menu.
   Or
   Press **F7**.

8. Enter your name (last name first) and press **Enter**. A new card appears with your name at the top.

9. Enter your telephone number(s) on the card.

### To Save and Exit the Cardfile

10. Choose **Save** from the **File** menu.

11. Choose **Exit** from the **File** menu. Cardfile closes.

►**ACTIVITY**

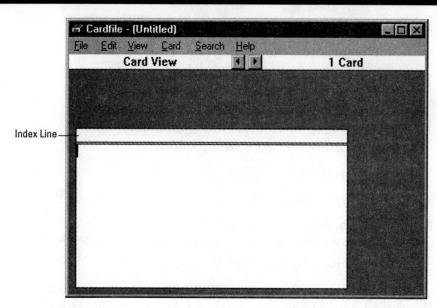

Index Line—

Figure 11-2 The Cardfile

1. Start the **Cardfile**.

2. Open **sampcrd.crd**.

3. Search for the card that contains the name **Clinchfield Bookstore**.

4. Close the Find box.

5. Choose **New** from the **File** menu.

6. Double-click the index line, as shown in Figure 11-2. You are given the opportunity to enter text for the index line of the card.

7. Enter your name on the index line and press **Enter**.

8. Key your address and telephone number on the card. Also include other means of contact, such as fax number, e-mail address, etc.

9. Add a card using the name of someone you know. If he or she has a company name, include that. Also include telephone numbers, etc.

10. Save the cardfile on your work disk as **MyFile.crd** and exit **Cardfile**.

# LESSON 109

## Using the Notepad

In this lesson, you will learn to use the Notepad. The Notepad is a simple text editor that has almost none of the features of a word processor.

## ►SKILL PRACTICE

**NOTE** The Notepad works with files that contain text only. No special formatting or fonts are available in Notepad. WordPad should be used for documents that require these features.

### To Start the Notepad

1. Start **Notepad** from the **Accessories** menu.

### To Open a Text File

2. Choose **Open** from the **File** menu.

3. Open the document named **Printing from an Icon** from your work disk. The text document appears.

### To Create a New File

4. Choose **New** from the **File** menu. The Notepad is cleared.

5. Choose **Word Wrap** from the **Edit** menu. The Word Wrap feature causes text to wrap within the boundaries of the window.

6. Enter the following text into the Notepad:

   ```
   Notepad is ideal for making lists or quick
   notes. Because Notepad starts quickly and
   uses less memory than a word processor, it
   works well for simple text that you access
   often, such as a "things to do" list.
   Notepad is also good for editing existing
   text files.
   ```

### To Save and Exit Notepad

7. Choose **Save As** from the **File** menu. Save the file on your work disk as **About Notepad**.

8. Choose **Exit** from the **File** menu. Notepad closes.

## ►ACTIVITY

1. Start **Notepad**.

2. Open the file you saved in the Skill Practice (**About Notepad**).

3. Add the following paragraph to the file:

   ```
   Notepad can also be used to prepare text
   to be e-mailed or distributed to others.
   Because Notepad saves files as simple
   text files, the files can be read by
   others no matter what word processor or
   text editor they use.
   ```

4. Save and print the file.

5. Exit **Notepad**.

# LESSON 110

**Playing a Music CD**

In this lesson, you will learn to play a music CD using the Windows 95 CD Player. If your computer system does not have a CD-ROM capable of playing music CDs, you will not be able to complete this lesson.

## ►SKILL PRACTICE

### To Start the CD Player

1. Click the **Start** button and access the **Accessories** menu.

2. Click **Multimedia** in the **Accessories** menu. The Multimedia menu appears.

3. Choose **CD Player** from the **Multimedia** menu. The CD Player appears, as shown in Figure 11-3.

Figure 11-3 CD Player

### To Play a Music CD

4. Insert the music CD into the CD-ROM drive.

5. Click the **Play** button. The CD begins to play.

6. Click the **Pause** button. The music pauses.

7. Click the **Pause** button again. The music resumes.

8. Click the **Stop** button. The music stops.

9. Choose **Exit** from the **Disc** menu. The CD Player closes.

## ►ACTIVITY

1.  Start the **CD Player**.
2.  If necessary, insert a music CD.
3.  Start playing with the third song.
4.  Stop the CD from playing.
5.  Exit the **CD Player**.

| Button | Description |
| --- | --- |
| | Allows you to enter the artist and title of the CD and choose which tracks to play |
| | Causes the time elapsed in the current song to be displayed |
| | Causes the time remaining in the current song to be displayed |
| | Causes the time remaining on the entire CD to be displayed |
| | Causes songs to be played in random order |
| | Causes the first song to repeat when end of CD is reached |
| | Causes only the first few seconds of each song to be played |
| | Moves to the previous song. If a song is playing, the button causes the song to begin at the beginning |
| | Moves backward in the current song |
| | Moves forward in the current song |
| | Moves to the next song |
| | Ejects the CD |

Table 11-2 describes the purpose of the other buttons on the CD Player.

LESSON
# 111

**Using the Media Player**

In this lesson, you will learn how to use the Media Player.

## ►SKILL PRACTICE

### To Start the Media Player

1. Click the **Start** button and access the **Accessories** menu.

2. Click **Multimedia** in the **Accessories** menu. The Multimedia menu appears.

3. Choose **Media Player** from the **Multimedia** menu. The Media Player appears (see Figure 11-4).

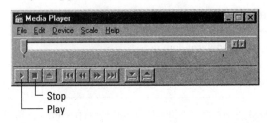

Figure 11-4 The Media Player

### To Play a Sound

4. Choose **Open** from the **File** menu. The Open dialog box appears.

5. If necessary, change to the **Media** folder in the **Windows** folder of the **C:** drive.

6. Select **The Microsoft Sound** and click **Open**.

7. Click the **Play** button (see Figure 11-4). The sound plays.

8. Exit the Media Player.

### To Play a Video Clip

9. Copy the file named **Win95** from your work disk to the desktop.

10. Start the Media Player.

11. Choose **Open** from the **File** menu. The Open dialog box appears.

12. Choose **Desktop** from the **Look in** box.

13. Choose **Video for Windows (*.avi)** from the **File of type:** box.

*(continued on next page)*

**NOTE** This lesson asks you to copy the video clip to the desktop because playing a video clip from floppy disk can result in delays in the presentation.

► **ACTIVITY**

*Skill Practice* (*continued*)

14. Select the file named **Win95** and click **Open**. A window appears, displaying the first frame of the video clip (see Figure 11-5).

Figure 11-5 Video Clip

15. Choose **Options** from the **Edit** menu.

16. If not already selected, select the **Auto Repeat** option.

17. Click **OK**.

18. Click the **Play** button. The video clip plays. Because you set the option to auto repeat, the clip plays continously.

19. Click the **Stop** button. The video clip stops.

20. Choose **Exit** from the **File** menu. The Media Player closes.

In this lesson, you will learn how to record sounds using the Sound Recorder. If your computer does not have a sound card that supports sound recording and a microphone, you will not be able to complete this lesson.

## ►SKILL PRACTICE

### To Start the Sound Recorder

1. Click the **Start** button and access the **Accessories** menu.

2. Click **Multimedia** in the **Accessories** menu. The Multimedia menu appears.

3. Choose **Sound Recorder** from the **Multimedia** menu. The Sound Recorder appears (see Figure 11-6).

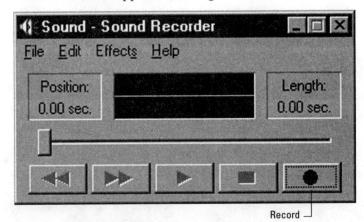

Figure 11-6 The Sound Recorder

### To Record a Sound

4. Click the **Record** button.

5. Speak into the microphone for about 3 seconds.

6. When you are finished speaking, click the **Stop** button.

### To Play a Sound

7. Click the **Play** button. The sound you just recorded plays.

8. Choose **Exit** from the **File** menu. There is no need to save. The Sound Recorder closes.

# 112

## ►ACTIVITY

1. Start the **Sound Recorder**.

2. Record your name.

3. Choose **Save As** from the **File** menu.

4. Save the sound on your work disk as **My Sound**.

5. Play the sound.

6. Exit the **Sound Recorder**.

# LESSON 113

Using the Run Command

In this lesson, you will learn how to run programs using the Run command.

---

## ►SKILL PRACTICE

### To Use the Run Command

You can use the Run command to start a program that is not on the Start menu, to start an installation program on a floppy disk, or to browse storage devices for a program.

1. Click the **Start** button.

2. Choose **Run** from the **Start** menu. The Run dialog box appears, as shown in Figure 11-7.

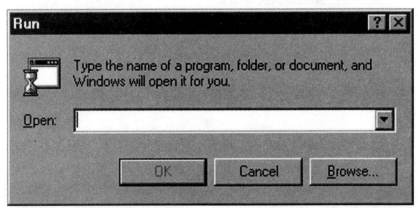

Figure 11-7 The Run Dialog Box

3. Key **Explorer** in the **Open** box and click **OK**. The Explorer starts.

4. Close the **Explorer**.

### To Browse for a Program

5. Click the **Start** button.

6. Choose **Run** from the **Start** menu.

7. Click **Browse**. The Browse dialog box appears.

8. Open the **Windows** folder on the **C:** drive.

9. Select **Calc** and click **Open**. The path and filename of the Calculator appear in the Run dialog box.

*(continued on next page)*

► **ACTIVITY**

1. Use the **Run** command to run the **Notepad**.
2. Exit **Notepad**.
3. Access the **Run** dialog box.
4. Click the arrow at the end of the **Open** box.
5. Run the **Calculator**.
6. Exit the **Calculator**.

*Skill Practice* (*continued*)

10. Click **OK**. The Calculator starts.

11. Close the **Calculator**.

## To Run a Recently Run Program

12. Access the **Run** dialog box.

13. Click the arrow at the end of the **Open** box. A list of recently run programs appears.

14. Choose **Explorer** and click **OK**.

15. Close the **Explorer**.

In this lesson, you will learn to make an application run at startup. This feature is useful when you have an application that you want to begin running as soon as your computer starts.

## ►SKILL PRACTICE

### To Make a Startup Program

To make a program start automatically when Windows 95 is loaded, put the application or a shortcut to the application in the Startup folder. You can also put a document or shortcut to a document in the Startup folder, and the document will be opened on startup.

This lesson assumes the Win95 video clip is still on the desktop.

1. Right-click the **Win95** video clip that appears on the desktop.

2. Choose Cut from the shortcut menu.

3. Right-click the **Start** button and choose **Open** from the shortcut menu. The Start Menu folder opens.

4. Open the **Programs** folder.

5. Open the **Startup** folder.

6. Choose **Paste** from the **Edit** menu in the Startup folder menu bar. The Win95 video clip is copied into the Startup folder.

7. Close all open windows.

8. Choose **Shut Down** from the **Start** menu.

9. Choose **Restart the computer** and click **Yes**. The computer restarts. When Windows reloads, the video clip automatically begins playing.

10. If necessary, close the video clip.

## ►ACTIVITY

1. Open the **Startup** folder.

2. Delete the **Win95** video clip from the **Startup** folder.

3. Leave the **Startup** folder open and open the **Windows** folder.

4. Create a shortcut to the **Calculator**.

5. Move the **Calculator** shortcut to the **Startup** folder.

6. Restart the computer. The **Calculator** starts automatically after Windows 95 reloads.

7. Delete the **Calculator** shortcut from the **Startup** folder.

8. Restart the computer.

# LESSON 115

**Introduction to the Control Panel**

In this lesson, you will learn how to access the Control Panel. You will also learn about the kinds of things the Control Panel controls.

## ►SKILL PRACTICE

**TIP**

The Control Panel can also be accessed from the Explorer. It is found on the same level as your storage devices.

### About the Control Panel

The Control Panel is a window that contains tools that allow you to control many features of Windows. Items in the Control Panel allow you to connect to hardware added to your system, add and remove Windows components, set display options, and more. The contents of the Control Panel will vary, depending on the kind of system you have and what programs you have installed.

### To Access the Control Panel

You can access the Control Panel from the Settings menu on the Start menu or from the My Computer window.

1. Click the **Start** button.

2. Access the **Settings** menu.

3. Choose **Control Panel** from the **Settings** menu. The Control Panel appears similar to Figure 12-1.

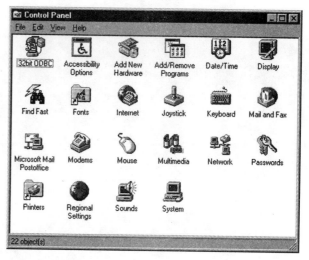

Figure 12-1 The Control Panel

4. Close the **Control Panel**.

*(continued on next page)*

LESSON

# 115

►**ACTIVITY**

1. Open the **Control Panel** from the **Start** menu.
2. Close the **Control Panel**.
3. Start the **Explorer** from the **Start** menu.
4. Scroll the left pane to find the **Control Panel** folder. If the My Computer icon is collapsed, you must expand it to make the Control Panel visible.
5. Click the **Control Panel** folder in the left pane. The Control Panel tools appear in the right pane.
6. Close the **Explorer**.

*Skill Practice* (continued)

5. Open the **My Computer** window. The Control Panel is accessible alongside your storage devices, as shown in Figure 12-2.

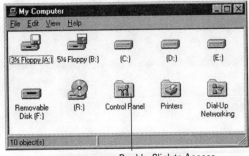

Double-Click to Access
the Control Panel

Figure 12-2 The Control Panel can be accessed from the My Computer window.

6. Double-click the **Control Panel** folder. The Control Panel appears.
7. Close the **Control Panel**.
8. Close the **My Computer** window.

**Using the Hardware Wizard**

In this lesson, you will learn about the Hardware Wizard.

## ►SKILL PRACTICE

You can use the Hardware Wizard to help you properly install devices. You can choose to manually select the new device even if the device is not yet installed. The Hardware Wizard will present you with recommended settings for the new device. You can use the recommended settings to configure the hardware you are installing and then run the Hardware Wizard again after the new hardware is installed.

Figure 12-3 The Add New Hardware Tool

### About the Hardware Wizard

The Hardware Wizard is a tool that communicates with your system's hardware to identify any hardware that has been added since Windows was installed. Use the Hardware Wizard after you add new devices to ensure that Windows has properly recognized the changes.

### To Run the Hardware Wizard

1. Click the **Start** button.
2. Access the **Settings** menu.
3. Choose **Control Panel** from the **Settings** menu. The Control Panel appears.
4. Double-click the **Add New Hardware** icon (see Figure 12-3). The Hardware Wizard appears.
5. Click **Next**. The second screen of the wizard appears, as shown in Figure 12-4.

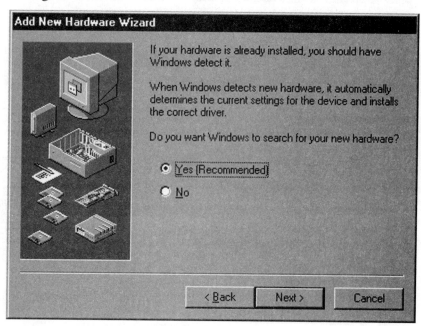

Figure 12-4 The Hardware Wizard

*(continued on next page)*

## ► ACTIVITY

Prepare a report outlining the hardware installed on your system. Include any specifications that you can determine. End the report with possibilities for upgrade of your system.

### *Skill Practice* (continued)

The Hardware Wizard leads you through a series of screens that detect your hardware and asks you for any necessary information. The detection process is lengthy and can occasionally cause the computer to become unresponsive. For these reasons, we will not continue with the Hardware Wizard in this lesson. Figure 12-5 shows the screen of the wizard that performs the hardware detection.

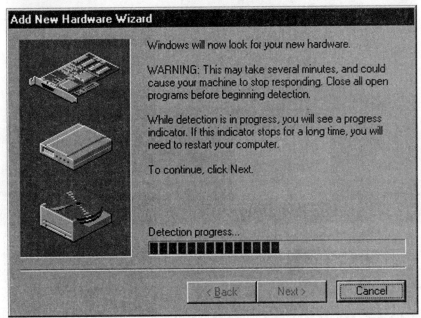

Figure 12-5 The Hardware Wizard automatically detects changes in the computer's hardware.

6. Click **Cancel**.

7. Close the **Control Panel**.

**UNIT 12**

**LESSON**
# 117
**Adding and Removing Programs and Windows Components**

In this lesson, you will learn how to add and remove programs and windows components using the Add/Remove Programs tool in the Control Panel.

## ►SKILL PRACTICE

## To Add or Remove Programs

1.  Open the **Control Panel**.

2.  Double-click **Add/Remove Programs**. The Add/Remove Programs Properties dialog box appears, as shown in Figure 12-6.

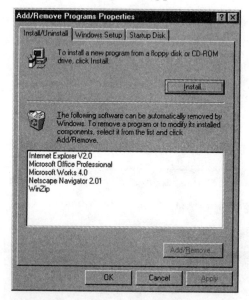

Figure 12-6 Install/Uninstall Programs

The Install button near the top right corner of the dialog box allows you to install new software from a floppy disk or CD-ROM. It will search the available floppy drives and CD-ROM drive for software to be installed. If none is found, a command prompt will appear to allow you to specify the path to the software or browse for it. The bottom portion of the dialog box lists software that can be uninstalled from the Control Panel.

## To Add or Remove Windows Components

3.  Click the **Windows Setup** tab of the dialog box. The dialog box appears similar to Figure 12-7.

*(continued on next page)*

►**ACTIVITY**

1. Open the **Control Panel**.

2. Double-click **Add/Remove Programs**.

3. If it is not already selected, click the **Windows Setup** tab of the dialog box.

4. Click the **Accessories** component to select it.

5. Click the **Details** button. Make a list of the **Accessories** components that are not currently installed on your system.

6. Click **Cancel** twice and close the **Control Panel**.

*Skill Practice* (continued)

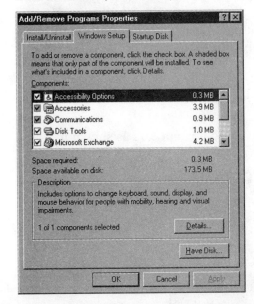

Figure 12-7 Windows Setup

The Components list shows the components of Windows 95 that are currently installed. The scrolling list displays categories of components. A check mark in a white box indicates that all components in that category are installed. No check mark indicates that none of the components in that category are installed. A check mark in a gray box indicates that some of the components in that category are installed.

To see the components in the highlighted category, click the Details button. Remove the check mark from any component you wish to remove and check the components you wish to add. Click OK to remove and/or add the components.

4. Click **Cancel**. The window closes.

5. Close the **Control Panel**.

# LESSON 118

**Display Settings and Appearance**

In this lesson, you will learn how to change display settings and appearance.

## ►SKILL PRACTICE

### To Change Display Settings

You can set the number of colors your screen will display and the size of the desktop area. Many programs will require that your display be set to a minimum of 256 colors. Desktop area is measured by the number of *pixels* (called the *resolution*) that will be used to create the screen. Higher resolutions cause the windows and text to appear smaller and more sharply defined.

1. Open the **Control Panel**.

2. Double-click **Display**. The Display Properties dialog box appears.

3. Click the **Settings** tab. The dialog box appears as shown in Figure 12-8.

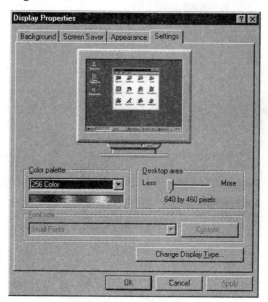

Figure 12-8 Display Properties Dialog Box

The number of colors displayed can be chosen in the Color palette. The display resolution can be selected by sliding the control under Desktop Area.

*(continued on next page)*

> **NOTE**
> The number of colors and the desktop area available will vary, depending on your monitor and video adapter.

## ►ACTIVITY

1. Experiment with the available color schemes.

2. Set the color scheme back to the **Windows Standard** color scheme.

3. Close the **Control Panel**.

*Skill Practice* (*continued*)

## To Change Color Scheme

4. Click the **Appearance** tab of the dialog box. The dialog box appears similar to Figure 12-9.

Figure 12-9 Display Appearance

The controls at the bottom of the dialog box allow you to select a color scheme or even select colors individually for each item on the display. The top of the dialog box shows a sample of the selected color scheme.

5. Choose **Wheat** from the **Scheme** box. The sample in the dialog box changes to the selected color scheme.

6. Click **OK**. The Display Properties dialog box closes, and the color scheme is applied.

7. Double-click **Display** in the Control Panel.

8. Click the **Appearance** tab.

9. Choose **Windows Standard** from the Scheme box. The sample in the dialog box shows the standard color selection.

10. Click **OK**. The standard color scheme is applied.

11. Leave the **Control Panel** open for the Activity that follows.

# LESSON 119

## Adding Desktop Patterns and Wallpaper

In this lesson, you will learn how to add desktop patterns and wallpaper. Patterns and wallpaper are a way to personalize your computer or make the desktop more attractive.

## ►SKILL PRACTICE

**NOTE**
Although both patterns and wallpaper add zest to the desktop, they are different. *Patterns* are simple lines and shapes that repeat to create a pattern on the screen. *Wallpaper* can be a graphic as large as the screen or smaller than the screen. Wallpaper can be centered on the screen or made to repeat like a pattern.

### To Apply a Pattern

1. Open the **Control Panel**.

2. Double-click **Display**. The Display Properties dialog box appears.

3. If necessary, click the **Background** tab. The dialog box appears as shown in Figure 12-10.

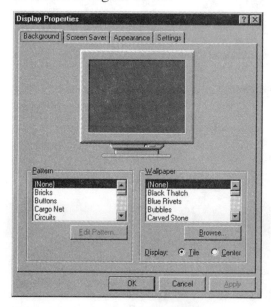

Figure 12-10 Display Backgrounds

4. If necessary, choose **[None]** from the **Wallpaper** list.

5. Choose **Circuits** from the **Pattern** list. A sample of the pattern appears in the graphic of the monitor that appears in the dialog box.

6. Click **Apply**. The pattern appears on the desktop.

7. Choose **Live Wire** from the **Pattern** list and click **OK**. The desktop pattern changes, and the dialog box closes.

*(continued on next page)*

► **ACTIVITY**

1. Experiment with the patterns and wallpapers available on your system.

2. Select a favorite pattern or wallpaper and leave it selected as you complete this unit.

*Skill Practice (continued)*

## To Apply a Wallpaper

8. Open the **Display Properties** dialog box.

9. Choose **[None]** from the **Pattern** list.

10. Choose **Clouds** from the **Wallpaper** list. A sample of the wallpaper appears in the graphic of the monitor.

11. Click **Apply**. The wallpaper appears on the desktop.

12. Close the **Display Properties** dialog box and the **Control Panel** to get a better view of the wallpaper.

13. Open the **Control Panel** and the **Display Properties** dialog box.

14. Choose **Metal Links** from the **Wallpaper** list.

15. If necessary, choose the **Tile** display option.

16. Click **Apply**. The wallpaper appears on the desktop.

17. Choose **[None]** from the **Wallpaper** list.

18. Click **OK**.

**TIP** Because wallpaper is just a standard bitmap graphic, it can be created or modified in Paint. Wallpaper files are saved in the Windows folder.

# LESSON 120

## Using a Screen Saver

In this lesson, you will learn how to use a screen saver. After your computer has set idle for a period of time, screen savers replace the contents of your screen with interesting pictures.

# ►SKILL PRACTICE

## To Choose a Screen Saver

1. Open the **Control Panel**.
2. Double-click **Display**. The Display dialog box appears.
3. Click the **Screen Saver** tab.
4. Choose **Curves and Colors** from the **Screen Saver** list box. The dialog box appears as shown in Figure 12-11.

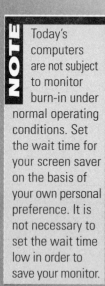

**NOTE** Today's computers are not subject to monitor burn-in under normal operating conditions. Set the wait time for your screen saver on the basis of your own personal preference. It is not necessary to set the wait time low in order to save your monitor.

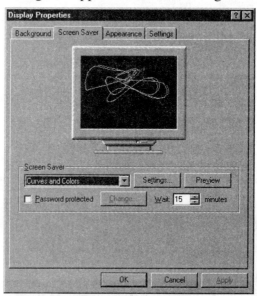

Figure 12-11 Choosing a Screen Saver

5. Click the **Settings** button. A dialog box of options for the Curves and Colors screen saver appears. The options will vary, depending on the screen saver selected.
6. Click **Cancel**.
7. Click **Preview** and do not move the mouse for a second or two. The screen saver appears as it will when activated.
8. Move the mouse to end the preview.
9. Double-click in the **Wait** text box and key **20**.
10. Preview some other screen savers available on your system.
11. Select your favorite screen saver and click **OK**.

## ►ACTIVITY

1. Make the **Scrolling Marquee** your screen saver.
2. Use the screen saver's settings to put the message **Windows 95** on the marquee.
3. Preview the screen saver.
4. Set the screen saver to **Flying Through Space** with a wait time of 15 minutes and click **OK**.

LESSON

# 121

**Changing Mouse Settings**

In this lesson, you will learn how to change mouse settings.

## ►SKILL PRACTICE

### To Change Button Configuration

1. Open the **Control Panel**.

2. Double-click **Mouse**. The Mouse Properties dialog box appears, as shown in Figure 12-12.

3. Choose either the right-handed or left-handed configuration. Choosing the left-handed configuration reverses the functions of the mouse buttons.

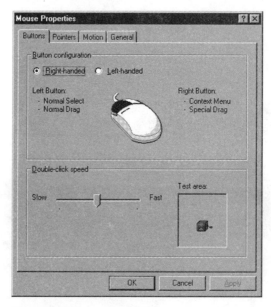

Figure 12-12 Mouse Properties

**NOTE**

If the double-click speed is too fast, it may be difficult to double click fast enough for the computer to recognize it. If the double-click speed is too slow, two clicks that were not intended to be a double-click may be interpreted as a double-click.

### To Change the Double-Click Speed

You can change the speed at which you must double click for Windows to recognize the two clicks as a double click.

4. Double-click in the **Test area**. The jack-in-the-box pops up.

5. Double-click in the **Test area** again. The jack-in-the-box goes back in the box.

6. Drag the double-click speed slider to its slowest setting.

*(continued on next page)*

## SKILL PRACTICE (continued)

7. Click twice in the **Test area**. Repeatedly double-click, each time clicking slower, until you find the speed of the current setting.

8. Drag the double-click speed slider near the fastest setting.

9. Double-click in the **Test area**. See if you can double-click fast enough for the fast setting.

10. Drag the double-click speed slider back to its original position or near the center of the range.

## To View the Mouse Pointers

The Pointers section of the dialog box allows you to change the appearance of the pointer.

11. Click the **Pointers** tab. The Pointers section of the dialog box appears, as shown in Figure 12-13. The pointer takes on a variety of shapes, depending on the current function.

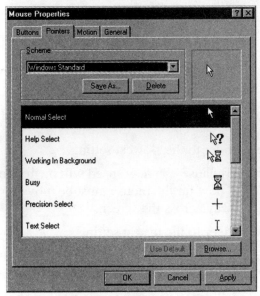

Figure 12-13 Customizing Pointers

12. Scroll through the list of pointer shapes.

*(continued on next page)*

**Changing Mouse
Settings**

►**SKILL PRACTICE** (continued)

## To Change Pointer Speed

13. Click the **Motion** tab. The Motion section of the dialog box appears, as shown in Figure 12-14.

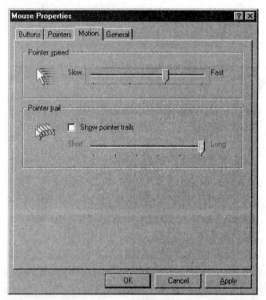

Figure 12-14 Customizing Mouse Motion

14. Drag the pointer speed slider to the slowest setting.

15. Click **Apply**. After a short pause, the new speed will be in effect. Move the pointer. Notice how far the mouse must be moved to move the pointer all the way across the screen.

16. Drag the pointer speed slider to the fastest setting.

17. Click **Apply**. Notice how quickly the pointer moves in response to even a slight movement of the mouse.

18. Return the pointer speed slider to its original position, or about the center of the range.

19. Click **Apply**.

*(continued on next page)*

## ►ACTIVITY

1. Change the double-click speed on your computer to the speed you feel most comfortable with.

2. Change the pointer speed to the fastest setting.

3. Turn on pointer trails.

4. Apply the changes by clicking **OK**.

5. Close all windows.

6. Open the **My Computer** window.

7. Open the **Control Panel**.

8. Return the mouse properties to their normal settings.

9. Close all windows.

*Skill Practice* (*continued*)

## To Turn on Pointer Trails

20. Click the **Show pointer trails** check box. If pointer trails are already on, leave them on for the steps that follow.

21. Move the pointer around the dialog box. Notice the trail of pointers that follows your pointer.

22. Click the **Show pointer trails** check box. The pointer trails are turned off.

23. Click **Cancel** to close the Mouse Properties dialog box.

**TIP** Pointer trails sometimes make the pointer easier to see on portable computers with liquid-crystal displays.

# LESSON 122

**Changing Date and Time**

In this lesson, you will learn how to change the system date and time.

## ►SKILL PRACTICE

### To Set the Date and Time

1. Open the **Control Panel**.

2. Double-click **Date/Time**. The Date/Time Properties dialog box appears, as shown in Figure 12-15.

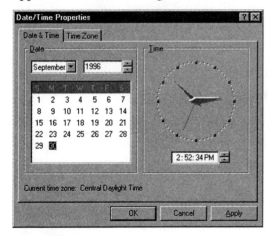

Figure 12-15 Date/Time Properties

3. Click the arrow at the end of the month text box. The month text box has a month selected but is not labeled.

4. Choose **June** from the month text box.

5. Click the **11** on the displayed calendar.

6. Double-click the hour on the digital time display.

7. Click the up arrow at the end of the digital time display to advance the hour.

8. Click **Cancel** to exit the dialog box without changing the date or time.

**NOTE**

The Time Zone tab of the Date/Time Properties dialog box allows you to set your time zone. You can also set an option that causes Windows to automatically adjust for daylight savings time.

► **ACTIVITY**

1. Use the **Date/Time Properties** dialog box to find out what day your birthday falls on in the year 2010.

2. Look at the calendar for February of 2012.

3. Cancel the **Date/Time Properties** dialog box and close the **Control Panel**.

LESSON
# 123

**Viewing Fonts**

In this lesson, you will learn how to view the fonts available on your system.

## ►SKILL PRACTICE

### To View the Installed Fonts

1. Open the **Control Panel**.

2. Double-click **Fonts**. The Fonts folder opens.

3. Choose **List Fonts by Similarity** from the **View** menu. A font box appears at the top of the window. Windows will compare the fonts in your system with the font selected in the font box.

4. Choose **Times New Roman** from the **List fonts by similarity to:** font box. The fonts in the window are ordered on the basis of their similarity to Times New Roman.

5. Choose **Hide Variations** from the **View** menu. The fonts that are simply style variations (such as bold, italic, and underline) of another font are hidden from view.

6. Scroll down, if necessary, to find the font named **Courier New**.

7. Double-click **Courier New**. A description and sample of the font appears, as shown in Figure 12-16.

Figure 12-16 Font Description and Sample

8. Click **Print**. The Print dialog box appears.

*(continued on next page)*

**NOTE** Deleting a font from the Font window deletes the font from the system. To install a new font, choose Install New Font from the File menu.

►**ACTIVITY**

1. Open the **Fonts** window.
2. List fonts by their similarity to **Arial**.
3. Print the description for **Times New Roman**.
4. Return the background pattern or wallpaper to the original setting.
5. Close all windows.

*Skill Practice* (*continued*)

9. Click **OK**. The description and sample print.

10. Click **Done**. The font description closes.

11. Close the **Fonts** window.

12. Close the **Control Panel**.

# LESSON 124

## Performing a Backup

In this lesson, you will learn how to use the Windows 95 backup program.

## ►SKILL PRACTICE

### To Perform a Backup

For this lesson, you will need a blank floppy disk or a disk that can be safely erased.

1. Create a folder on the **C:** drive named **My Work**.

2. If not already in the floppy drive, insert your work disk.

3. Copy the contents of your work disk to the **My Work** folder on the C: drive.

4. Remove your work disk from the floppy disk drive.

5. Insert a blank disk or a disk that can be safely erased.

6. If the floppy disk is not blank or is unformatted, format the floppy disk.

7. Click the **Start** button. Click **Programs**, then **Accessories**, and then **System Tools**.

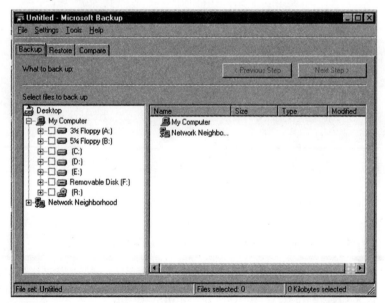

Figure 13-1 Microsoft Backup

*(continued on next page)*

► **ACTIVITY**

1. Use the Quick format option to erase the floppy diskette you used in the Skill Practice.

2. Backup the **My Work** folder from the C: drive to the floppy diskette. Name the backup **Work Folder**.

3. When the backup is complete, exit backup.

4. Use **My Computer** to view the contents of the floppy disk. You will see the file created by Backup.

5. Close all open windows and remove the backup disk.

*Skill Practice* (continued)

8. Choose **Backup** from the **System Tools** menu. Backup starts. If a welcome message appears, click **OK** to dismiss the message. You may also see another message informing you that a backup set has been created for you. Click **OK** to dismiss this message.

9. If necessary, click the **Backup** tab in the Microsoft Backup window. The window should appear similar to Figure 13-1. The backup window has an appearance similar to the Explorer.

10. In the left pane, click the icon that represents your **C:** drive. Do not click the check box next to the icon. The folders on the C: drive will appear in the right pane.

11. In the right pane, click the check box next to the **My Work** folder. The contents of the My Work folder are selected for backup.

12. Click the **Next Step >** button. You must now specify the drive that will receive the backup.

13. Click the icon that represents the floppy disk drive that holds the blank disk.

14. Click the **Start Backup** button. You are prompted for a name for the backup.

15. Key **My Work** and click **OK**. The backup begins.

16. When the backup is complete, a message box appears indicating that the backup has been completed. Click **OK** to close the message box.

17. Click **OK** to close the backup summary. The Microsoft Backup window appears.

18. Remove the backup disk and choose **Exit** from the **File** menu.

**NOTE** If you click a check box next to a device in the left pane, the entire disk will be selected for backup.

**NOTE** If a backup requires more than one floppy disk, Microsoft Backup will prompt you for subsequent disks.

LESSON
# 125

**Restoring a Backup**

In this lesson, you will learn how to restore files from a backup.

# ►SKILL PRACTICE

For this lesson, you will need the floppy disk that contains the backup created in the previous lesson.

## To Restore a Backup

1. Delete the folder on the **C:** drive named **My Work**.

2. Click the **Start** button. Click **Programs**, then **Accessories**, and then **System Tools**.

3. Choose **Backup** from the **System Tools** menu. Backup starts. As in the previous lesson, if a welcome message appears, click **OK** to dismiss the message. If you see another message informing you that a backup set has been created for you, click **OK** to dismiss this message.

4. Click the **Restore** tab in the Microsoft Backup window. The window should appear similar to Figure 13-2.

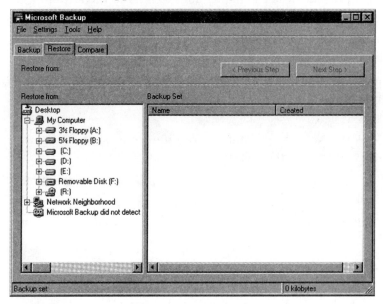

Figure 13-2 Restoring a Backup

5. Insert the floppy disk that you backed up in the previous lesson.

*(continued on next page)*

***Skill Practice*** *(continued)*

6. In the left pane, click the icon that represents the floppy drive that holds your backup disk. The *My Work* backup will appear in the right pane.

7. In the right pane, click the **Work Folder** backup set.

8. Click the **Next Step >** button. After a few moments, the contents of the backup set will be read. In the left pane you will see the folders of the backup.

9. Click the check box next to the **My Work** folder in the left pane. The files that were backed up appear in the right pane. All the files should have a check mark by them.

10. Click the **Start Restore** button. The My Work folder and the files it contains will begin to be restored to the C: drive. The status of the restore will be shown in a status window like the one in Figure 13-3.

11. When the restore is complete, a message box appears indicating that the backup has been completed. Click **OK** to close the message box.

12. Click **OK** to close the Restore window. The Microsoft Backup window appears.

13. Remove the backup disk from the floppy drive.

14. Choose **Exit** from the **File** menu.

15. Using **My Computer** or the **Explorer**, verify that the My Work folder has been restored to the C: drive.

16. Close all open windows.

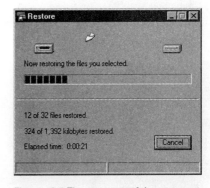

Figure 13-3 The progress of the restore process is shown in the status window.

 Removing the check mark from a file in the right pane will prevent it from being restored.

In this lesson, you will learn how to use the disk defragmenter. The disk defragmenter reorganizes the data on a disk and puts together any files that are stored on the disk in fragments rather than in one piece.

## ►SKILL PRACTICE

For this lesson, you will need the floppy disk used in the previous two lessons.

### To Defragment a Disk

1. Insert the backup disk you used in the previous two lessons.

2. Delete the backup set from the floppy disk.

3. Copy the **My Work** folder from the **C:** drive to the floppy disk.

4. Open the floppy disk window and then open the **My Work** folder.

5. Delete the **More Documents** folder and the **Reports** folder from the **My Work** folder on the floppy disk.

6. Click the **Start** button. Click **Programs**, then **Accessories** and then **System Tools**.

7. Choose **Disk Defragmenter** from the **System Tools** menu. The Defragmenter starts. The first window prompts you for the storage device you want to defragment.

8. Choose the drive that holds your floppy disk and click **OK**. You may get a message indicating that the disk does not need to be defragmented. If you get that message, click **Start** to start the defragmenter anyway. The defragmenter begins working.

9. Click **Show Details**. The screen expands to show a map of the contents of your drive. Your screen should appear similar to Figure 13-4.

10. While the defragmenter works, click the **Legend** button to display a window that explains the map on your screen.

11. Click **Close** to close the Legend.

12. When the defragmenter is complete, you will be asked if you wish to quit. Click **Yes**. The Disk Defragmenter quits.

**NOTE** The deletion of these folders leaves blank areas in the data on the floppy disk. The Disk Defragmenter will consolidate the free space on the disk.

## ►ACTIVITY

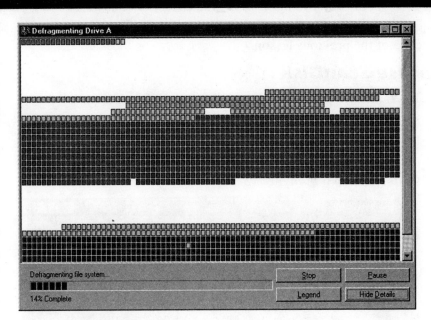

Figure 13-4 Defragmenting

1. Start the **Disk Defragmenter**.

2. Use the Disk Defragmenter to defragment and optimize the free space on your work disk.

3. Quit the **Disk Defragmenter**.

U N I T

13

LESSON

# 127

Using ScanDisk

In this lesson, you will learn how to use ScanDisk to check disks for problems.

## ►SKILL PRACTICE

For this lesson, you will need the floppy disk used in the Skill Practice of the previous lesson.

### To Use ScanDisk

1. Insert the disk you used in the Skill Practice of the previous lesson.

2. Click the **Start** button. Click **Programs**, then **Accessories**, and then **System Tools**.

3. Choose **ScanDisk** from the **System Tools** menu. ScanDisk starts, as shown in Figure 13-5.

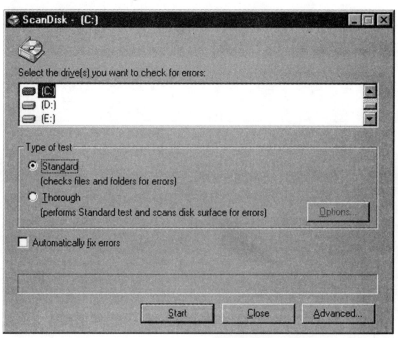

Figure 13-5 ScanDisk

> **NOTE**
>
> If errors are found during a scan, you will be asked if you want to repair the problems. If you select the Automatically fix errors check box, errors will be fixed without prompting you for instructions.

4. From the list of storage devices at the top of the ScanDisk window, select the floppy drive that holds the disk you used in the previous lesson. You may have to scroll the list up to see the appropriate drive.

*(continued on next page)*

## ►ACTIVITY

1. Start **ScanDisk**.

2. Perform a standard scan on the **C:** drive. If problems are reported, consult your instructor.

3. Use **Alt + Print Screen** to capture the window that provides the results of the scan.

4. Close **ScanDisk**.

5. Start **Paint**.

6. Paste the captured window into Paint and print it.

7. Exit **Paint**.

*Skill Practice (continued)*

5. If necessary, click the **Standard** scan option.

6. Click **Start**. ScanDisk begins analyzing the floppy disk. After a few moments, a window will appear summarizing the findings of the scan.

7. Click **Close**.

8. Click **Close** to close ScanDisk.

LESSON
# 128

**Checking the Properties of a Storage Device**

In this lesson, you will learn how to check the properties of a storage device.

## ►SKILL PRACTICE

### To Check the Properties of a Storage Device

1. Open the **My Computer** window.

2. Right-click the icon that represents your **C:** drive. A shortcut menu appears.

3. Choose **Properties** from the shortcut menu. The properties for the C: drive appear, as shown in Figure 13-6. The pie graph shows the amount of space used and free on the disk.

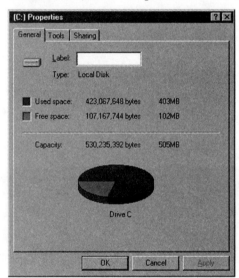

Figure 13-6 Disk Properties

4. Click the **Tools** tab at the top of the dialog box. The Tools section reminds you of how long it has been since you ran ScanDisk, backed up, or defragmented the disk. You can launch each of these system maintenance tools from this dialog box.

5. Click **Cancel** to close the dialog box.

## ►ACTIVITY

1. Look at the properties of other devices available on your system.

2. If necessary, insert a floppy disk and check its properties.

3. Close all open windows.

LESSON
# 129

**Running MS-DOS
Programs**

In this lesson, you will learn how to run MS-DOS programs from Windows 95.

## ►SKILL PRACTICE

### To Run an MS-DOS Program from My Computer or the Explorer

1.  Open the **My Computer** window.

2.  If necessary, insert your work disk into the floppy disk drive.

3.  Display the contents of your work disk.

4.  Double-click the MS-DOS program on your work disk called **Mileage**. A window appears, and the program begins to run, as shown in Figure 13-7.

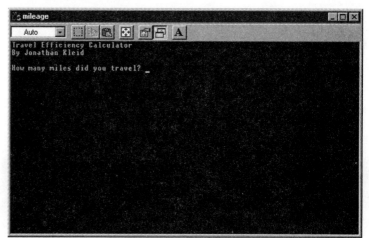

Figure 13-7 An MS-DOS Window

5.  Key **100** when prompted for miles and then press **Enter**.

6.  Key **4.34** when prompted for the number of gallons used. Press **Enter**.

7.  Enter the most recent gas price you have seen. The results of the analysis will appear. Notice the title bar now indicates that the program is finished.

8.  Click the close button to close the window.

*(continued on next page)*

# ►ACTIVITY

1. Run the MS-DOS program on your work disk called **Temperature Converter** by double-clicking its icon.

2. Enter a temperature in Celsius, and the program returns the temperature in Fahrenheit degrees.

3. Close the program window.

*Skill Practice* (*continued*)

## To Run a Program from the MS-DOS Prompt

9. Click the **Start** button.

10. Choose **MS-DOS Prompt** from the **Programs** menu. A DOS prompt appears.

11. Key either **A:\mileage** or **B:\mileage** (depending on the drive that holds your work disk) and press **Enter**. The Mileage program runs.

12. Enter realistic values when prompted. When the program finishes, you will again see a DOS prompt.

13. Key **exit** and press **Enter**. The window closes.

14. Close all open windows.

# LESSON 130

**Copying Between MS-DOS and Windows Programs**

In this lesson, you will learn how to run copy text from an MS-DOS program to a Windows 95 program.

## ►SKILL PRACTICE

### To Copy Between MS-DOS and Windows

1. Open the **My Computer** window.

2. If necessary, insert your work disk into the floppy disk drive.

3. Display the contents of your work disk.

4. Double-click the MS-DOS program on your work disk called **Mileage**. A window appears, and the program begins to run.

5. Enter realistic values in response to the questions asked by the program. When the program finishes, do not close the window.

6. Click the **Mark** button (see Figure 13-8). A blinking block cursor appears in the upper-left corner of the window.

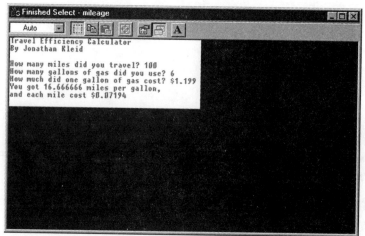

Figure 13-8 The Mark button allows you to copy text from a DOS window.

7. Drag the mouse from the blinking cursor to highlight the entire text in the window.

8. Click the **Copy** button.

9. Close the **Mileage** program window.

10. Start **WordPad**.

11. When WordPad's blank document appears, paste the text into the document.

12. Save the document on your work disk as **DOS Text**, print, and close.

## ►ACTIVITY

1. Choose **MS-DOS Prompt** from the **Programs** menu.

2. Key **DIR** at the MS-DOS prompt and press **Enter**.

3. Click the **Mark** button and copy the entire window of text.

4. Key **exit** and press **Enter**.

5. Start **Notepad**.

6. Paste the text into Notepad.

7. Save the document on your work disk as **DOS Directory**.

8. Print and close the **Notepad**.

## NETWORKING

Computers are much more useful and interesting when they work together. Computers communicate with each other using connections called *networks*. There are different kinds of computer networks. Many networks consist of just a few machines connected to each other within an office or building. Other networks may connect all of the computers in a large corporation. The Internet connects computers all over the world.

By definition, a network is two or more computers which have been linked together for the purpose of sharing information or resources. Computers can form a network over phone lines using a device called a modem. Computers can also form a network through other kinds of connections, including cables and satellite links.

## NETWORKING WITH WINDOWS 95

Windows 95 includes software to make networking easy. If your computer is connected to other computers in the same room or nearby, you are on a type of network called a *local area network* or *LAN*. Windows 95 includes software that allows you to share storage devices and printers over a local area network. For example, you can cause a specific folder on your hard disk to be accessible to other computers on the network. You can even require a password before access to the folder is allowed.

Another way Windows 95 assists with networking is by providing the software necessary to connect to other computers over a modem. Using Windows 95, you can also connect to online services such as America Online, CompuServe, and the Microsoft Network.

## THE MICROSOFT NETWORK

The Microsoft Network (MSN) is an online service provided by Microsoft. MSN provides its members with access to the Internet, electronic mail, news, product support, and more. The Microsoft Network's interface is similar to the Windows 95 interface. Browsing through the MSN is like browsing with the Explorer.

To start MSN, double-click the Microsoft Network icon on the desktop. If your Microsoft Network icon is labeled Setup the Microsoft Network, the Microsoft Network has not been set up. The first time you access MSN, you will be asked for your name and address, you will choose your member identification, and you must specify a way to pay for the service. You will also choose local access numbers which MSN will use for subsequent connections.

After you are a member, double-clicking the Microsoft Network icon will display a window for signing on similar to the one in Figure A-1.

Figure A-1 The Microsoft Network sign in screen

The Microsoft Network features a variety of areas, all of which can be accessed from MSN Central (see Figure A-2). MSN Central is the main menu for the Microsoft Network. From MSN Central, you can access MSN Today (a screen which highlights new features, gives the top news story, provides access to the events calendar, and more), manage e-mail, go to your favorite places, receive member assistance, or go to the categories of information within MSN.

# Appendix A

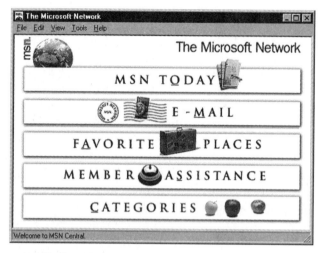

Figure A-2 MSN Central

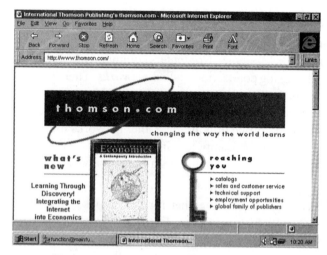

Figure A-3 The Microsoft Internet Explorer

## THE WORLD WIDE WEB

The World Wide Web (WWW) is the most popular way to use the Internet. The World Wide Web provides a graphical interface which links specially formatted documents all over the Internet. These documents provide information about people, institutions, businesses, research, and more. The graphical interface makes accessing the information easy.

To access WWW, you need a service provider that allows access to the Internet. A service provider is a company or school that provides the link between your computer and the Internet. Most people connect to the service provider via modem. In a school or business, however, you may have access over connections which are much faster than a modem. These faster lines are now available to homes as well.

Once you have Internet access, you need a Web browser such as Netscape, Mosaic, or the Microsoft Internet Explorer. Figure A-3 shows the Internet Explorer in action.

Documents on the World Wide Web are called *Web pages*. Each Web page has an address. Web addresses begin with http://, which is actually information for your Web browser, rather than part of the actual address. The http:// tells your web browser that the document at the address you are accessing should be treated as a Web page. Web documents are created using commands that tell your Web browser how to format the document on your screen. These commands also load pictures and provide links to other Web pages. The language of Web pages is called HyperText Markup Language (HTML).

An example of a complete Web address is http://www.thomson.com. Following the http:// is the address of the Web page. Many Web pages include www as part of their address. This is not necessary, however. Other characters may take the place of www. Web addresses do, however, end with a domain name and zone. In the example above, thomson is the domain name (the name of the computer). The zone in our example is com, which indicates that the site is commercial. Other commonly seen zones are edu (educational site) and gov (governmental site).

# Appendix B

## INTRODUCTION TO THE ACCESSIBILITY OPTIONS

Having an impairment of vision, sound, or dexterity can sometimes make it difficult to operate a computer effectively. Microsoft kept this in mind when creating Windows 95 by including special features called accessibility options. For example, there are options to make the keyboard easier to use and to allow you to use the keyboard in place of the mouse. Other options allow you to change the colors to high contrast colors, and increase the font size of the Windows' environment.

The Accessibility Options are accessed from the Control Panel. The Accessibility Properties dialog box appears as shown in Figure B-1. The five sections of the dialog box (Keyboard, Sound, Display, Mouse, and General) each contain options to make using the computer easier.

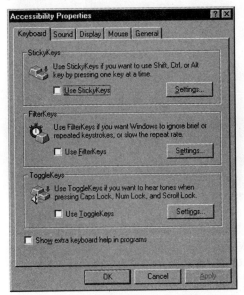

Figure B-1 Keyboard options of the Accessibility Properties dialog box

## KEYBOARD OPTIONS

The Keyboard section of the Accessibility Properties dialog box contains three options that will help people with dexterity impairments issue commands more easily.

### StickyKeys

The StickyKeys option makes entering key combinations such as Ctrl+C easier. When the Use StickyKeys option is checked, Windows begins treating the function keys (Shift, Ctrl, and Alt) as "sticky." This means that to issue a command, the user simply has to press one of the function keys and then release it. Windows keeps this key active until another key is pressed, making it possible to issue a command without pressing two keys simultaneously. The Settings button in this section give you more options for controlling the way StickyKeys are used.

### FilterKeys

By clicking the Use FilterKeys option, you can make Windows ignore repeated keystrokes, or make Windows slow down the repeat rate of letters. This makes it possible for Windows to recognize when the user is wanting to repeat a character, or is accidentally holding a key down too long. The Settings button on the right side of this section allows you to adjust the sensitivity of FilterKeys.

### ToggleKeys

The ToggleKeys option makes Windows produce a sound when the Caps Lock, Num Lock, or Scroll Lock keys are pressed. A high-pitched sound indicates that the lock is being turned on. A low-pitched sound indicates that the lock is being turned off. This is useful for those who have difficulty seeing the small lights on the keyboard.

## SOUND OPTIONS

Users who are hearing impaired can be assisted by the options in the Sound section of the Accessibility Properties dialog box (see Figure B-2).

# Appendix B

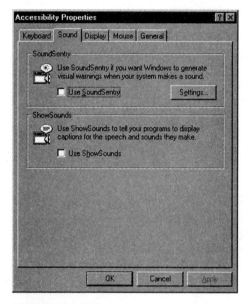

Figure B-2 Sound Options

### SoundSentry

The SoundSentry replaces the usual beep that the computer's speaker produces with a flash of a selected screen element. The Settings button allows you to choose the part of the screen which you want to flash.

### ShowSounds

Programs which are written to support the ShowSounds option will display text or icons in the place of sounds when the ShowSounds option is on.

## DISPLAY OPTIONS

For people with a vision disability, seeing the text on the screen can be very difficult. The Display section of Accessibility Options helps with this problem by allowing the user to make the text larger and the colors high contrast. By checking the Use High Contrast option, Windows will change its settings to make almost everything easier to read. The Settings button on the right opens a dialog box which allows the user to adjust the color scheme which Windows displays. It also lets you activate the shortcut to toggle this option on and off.

## MOUSE OPTIONS

Windows 95 was designed to be used with a mouse or other pointing device. Those who have difficulty manipulating a mouse may use the mouse options to cause the numeric keypad to move the mouse pointer and to perform clicks and dragging. The Use MouseKeys option (see Figure B-3) causes the arrows on the numeric keypad to move the mouse pointer. The 5 key performs a click, and the plus key (+) on the numeric keypad performs a double-click. The Ins key begins dragging and the Del key ends a drag operation.

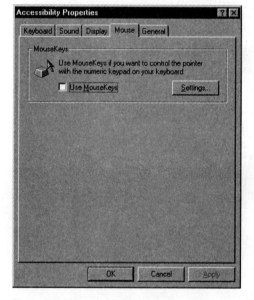

Figure B-3 Mouse options

The Settings button gives the user the ability to change the speed at which the cursor moves when an arrow key is pushed, along with the ability to use a shortcut to switch between the mouse and the keyboard.

## GENERAL OPTIONS

The General options apply to the administration of the Accessibility Options (see Figure B-4). The Automatic reset option causes the accessibility options to turn off after the computer has been idle for a specified length of time. The Notification option provides a message if any accessibility option is turned on or off using a shortcut key. The Notification option may prevent accessibility options from being turned on or off accidentally. The SerialKey devices option allows alternative input devices to have access to the computer if they are unable to use a standard keyboard or mouse. With the Settings button you can choose the port, and the speed at which this input device will operate. The device must be a SerialKey compatible device.

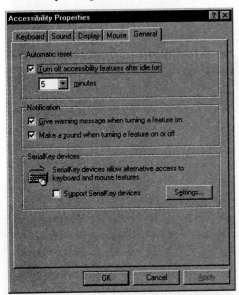

Figure B-4 General Options

# Glossary

**ANNOTATE** • To add a note to a Help topic.

**APPLICATION SOFTWARE** • The programs that perform useful tasks for the user.

**BOOK** • A category of Help topics.

**CASCADE** • To arrange and resize windows in such a way as to stack them neatly on top of each other with the title bars showing.

**CD-ROM DRIVE** • A device that allows computers to access data stored on compact disc.

**CENTRAL PROCESSING UNIT (CPU)** • The device that is the brain of the computer.

**CHECK BOX** • A dialog box control which allows you to choose one or more of a group of options.

**CLICK** • To quickly press and release the left mouse button.

**CLIPBOARD** • The area in the computer's memory where text that has been cut or copied is held.

**COMMAND BUTTONS** • Buttons which carry out commands.

**CURSOR** • The blinking vertical line that indicates the position at which the next character keyed will appear.

**DESKTOP** • The background against which the windows and icons appear.

**DIALOG BOX** • A window which provides information to the user or asks the user to supply more information.

**DOUBLE-CLICK** • To quickly press and release the mouse button twice in rapid succession.

**DRAG** • To press and hold the mouse button while moving the mouse pointer.

**DRAG AND DROP** • Dragging an item from one location to another to perform an operation.

**FAX MODEM** • A device that allows computers to communicate and send and receive faxes via telephone lines.

**FILE** • A program or document stored on a computer's storage device.

**FOLDER** • An item used to organize files into groups.

**FONT** • A typeface or design of type.

**GRAPHICAL USER INTERFACE (GUI)** • A way of interacting with a computer through graphic images and controls.

**HARDWARE** • The devices that make up a computer system.

**HIDDEN FILES AND FOLDERS** • Files and folders that are usually hidden from view.

**ICONS** • Tiny pictures used to represent files and to identify controls.

**KEYBOARD** • The device used to input text and numbers into the computer.

**LANDSCAPE ORIENTATION** • Printing text sideways on the page.

**LIST BOX** • A dialog box control which allows you to choose an item from a scrolling list.

**MARGIN** • The space between the edge of the page and the printed text.

**MAXIMIZE BUTTON** • Expands a window to fill the screen.

**MENU BAR** • The bar below the title bar from which menus pull down.

**MONITOR** • The computer's video display.

**MOUSE** • A hand-held input device that allows you to point and select items on the screen.

**MULTIMEDIA APPLICATIONS** • Programs that combine text, graphics, and sound.

**OPERATING SYSTEM** • The system software required to run an entire computer system.

**OPTION BUTTONS** • A dialog box control which allows you to choose only one of a group of options.

**PATH** • The drive letter and directories that lead to a particular file.

**PATTERNS** • simple lines or shapes that repeat to create a visual display on the screen.

**PICA** • A unit of measurement that equals 1/72 of an inch.

**PIXELS** • The dots that make up the picture on a computer screen.

**POINT** • A unit of measurement that equals 1/6 of an inch.

**POINT** • To position the mouse pointer on an icon or control on the screen.

**PORTRAIT ORIENTATION** • Printing text upright on the page, in the normal reading position.

**PRINTER** • An output device that puts text and images on paper.

**RANDOM ACCESS MEMORY (RAM)** • A computer's temporary storage.

**RESOLUTION** • A measurement of the number of dots that make up the screen.

**RESTORE BUTTON** • Returns a maximized window to the size it was before being maximized.

**RIGHT-CLICK** • To quickly press and release the right mouse button.

**SCROLL** • To move the contents of a window within the bounds of the window's size.

# Glossary

**SCROLL BARS** • Graphic elements which allow you to scroll the contents of a window.

**SELECT** • To highlight text in order to perform operations on it.

**SOFTWARE** • The instructions a computer follows.

**STYLE** • Variations in the appearance of text, such as bolding, underlining, and italics.

**SYSTEM SOFTWARE** • The software needed to control the hardware and load application software.

**SYSTEM UNIT** • The case that holds the processing unit and storage devices of the computer.

**TASKBAR** • The bar that displays the Start button, as well as buttons for each open program and window.

**TEXT BOX** • A dialog box control which allows you to key text in response to a question.

**TILE** • To arrange and resize windows in such a way as to make all of the windows fully visible at the same time.

**WALLPAPER** • a graphic element that can be as large as or smaller than the screen.

**WRITE-PROTECT** • To protect the contents of a disk by preventing the computer from making changes to the disk.

# Index

# Index

# Index

# Index